SIMPLE
CAFÉ FOOD

PENGUIN
BOOKS

SIMPLE
CAFÉ FOOD

SECRETS FROM THE
GARNET ROAD FOODSTORE

Julie Le Clerc

Photography by Shaun Cato-Symonds

Penguin Books

PENGUIN BOOKS

Penguin Books (NZ) Ltd, cnr Airborne and Rosedale Roads, Albany,
Auckland 1310, New Zealand
Penguin Books Ltd, 27 Wrights Lane, London W8 5TZ, England
Penguin Putnam Inc, 375 Hudson Street, New York, NY 10014, United States
Penguin Books Australia Ltd, 487 Maroondah Highway, Ringwood, Australia 3134
Penguin Books Canada Ltd, 10 Alcorn Avenue, Toronto, Ontario, Canada M4V 3B2
Penguin Books (South Africa) Pty Ltd, 4 Pallinghurst Road, Parktown,
Johannesburg 2193, South Africa
Penguin Books India (P) Ltd, 11, Community Centre, Panchsheel Park,
New Delhi 110 017, India

Penguin Books Ltd, Registered Offices: Harmondsworth, Middlesex, England

First published by Penguin Books (NZ) Ltd, 1999

5 7 9 10 8 6

Copyright © text, Julie Le Clerc, 1999
Copyright © photographs, Shaun Cato-Symonds, 1999

The right of Julie Le Clerc to be identified as the author of this work in terms of section 96 of the
Copyright Act 1994 is hereby asserted.

Designed and typeset by Seven
Printed by Condor Production, Hong Kong

ACKNOWLEDGEMENTS

To own and cook for a busy café takes dedication and the support of many. I am fortunate to have found both in my fellow workers and in those who frequent the Garnet Road Foodstore. This book has therefore evolved with the help and inspiration of many individuals to whom I give thanks.

I would like to thank our loyal customers for their continued support in making such a unique place possible. It has been my pleasure to meet you and to cook for you.

Deep and special thanks go to Helen – my greatest friend, an exceptional barista, second chef, and constant source of strength and comfort.

Thanks to all my loyal and committed staff, past and present, who have helped me through some pretty crazy times. Café working life can be fulfilling, entertaining and fun, and we have had a lot of laughs. It can also be very demanding and plain hard work. Teamwork has made all the difference, I could not have done this without you all and I am indebted. I greatly value your ongoing friendships.

I am grateful to my local purveyors/suppliers both for your products and for your supportive friendships and advice. I admire your commitment to providing quality ingredients, which of course are the essence of good cooking.

My thanks to Rachel Carley for making the most lovely china platters and bowls. It is a pleasure to serve food in such exquisite vessels.

Thank you to Michael Gifkins, my literary agent, for making your remarkable professional expertise, brilliance and extraordinary passion available to me in a number of ways. And for holding my hand ever so gently while I navigated the new and unfamiliar territory of cookbook writing.

Thank you Bernice and Philippa at Penguin Books (NZ) Ltd for your great enthusiasm, style and grace, and for Penguin's commitment to this book.

To Shaun Cato-Symonds for your most stunningly beautiful photography and for being so compatible to work with. Your true artistry has contributed another dimension to my work.

To Gideon Keith, for bringing your design skills to bear and putting it all together.

To ACP for producing beautiful magazines in which some of these recipes have previously appeared.

Thank you Mary and Gerard of Egan-Reid Ltd for your guiding push to begin this book in the first place.

An extra-special acknowledgement goes to my family and friends. Your encouragement, support and love mean so much.

INTRODUCTION

This book is a celebration of café style – the food, of course, but also the lifestyle. Café food is less intricate than restaurant food and yet a little more than everyday cooking. In café food you will find eclectic dishes blending tastes and accents, surprising combinations and seductive presentation. Often scaled down to become easily achievable, these innovative recipes are fun to experience.

The café lifestyle has been embraced by many urban dwellers and is now a part of life that most would find hard to give up. Brunch on the weekends, great espresso any time, pavement seating to watch the world go by, business lunches, family times, and stylish flavoursome meals, all enrich the lives of café habitués.

The Garnet Road Foodstore is my contribution to café style. For me, good food and ambience are of the utmost importance so I created a space where people could feel comfortable and at home while enjoying something to eat. Locals and now others from far and wide take pleasure from this neighbourhood eatery and I have been greatly rewarded by my customers' appreciation and support.

For as long as I can remember I have been curious about all things culinary. Cooking for me is now a bit of an obsession, a compelling addiction that drives me to create, sometimes at the oddest of times. I am constantly learning and as a result my recipes are continually evolving. I strive to compose full, clear flavours; honest food, which tastes of itself. My cooking is partly inspired or invented but essentially based on good-quality ingredients cooked well. Delicious and straightforward to prepare, this is food I hope you will all want to cook and eat.

The relaxed feel of simple café food also applies to cooking from this book. It is not full of impossible formulas since following rigid recipes takes all the joy out of cooking. So relax. Use these recipes as a base for your own ideas, add whatever takes your fancy and leave out parts or make substitutes if you wish. Begin to experiment and adapt recipes to what you have on hand as I do in the café kitchen.

Enjoy building an understanding of ingredients and methods, and sharing cooking. Take time to choose and prepare ingredients and time to enjoy cooking them well. When shopping, observe the principles of all good eateries – place enormous emphasis on using the best produce and insist on freshness and quality. Take advantage of the seasons to derive the fullest flavour from fruit and vegetables.

Food is one of our greatest sensual pleasures and is extremely evocative; the lasting taste of good food lingers in the memory for all time. Always enjoy the ritual of eating for it nourishes both body and soul. Remember the importance of presentation and use your treasured possessions to entertain and toast family and friendships. Have fun constructing food on a plate and employ the luscious use of colour to stimulate the appetite. Incorporating simple café food into your repertoire will enliven your everyday meals as well as special-occasion cooking.

The Garnet Road Foodstore has been a remarkable business and through many ups and downs still remains the stuff that dreams are made of: honest cooking, loyal and committed people, great times, hard work, hysterical moments and for me the fondest of memories. These recipes are a distillation of my years in the café kitchen. The café scene has taken on a momentum all of its own; this book is intended to help you catch it, to become consumed with a passion to cook and present simple café food in your own home.

Caramelised Onions with Roasted
Asparagus and Pickled Vegetables

<u>1</u> ANTIPASTI

Small dishes eaten before a meal are known in Italy as antipasti. In New Zealand, platters of antipasto ingredients are appropriate for many occasions. In the café and at home it is good to keep some antipasti ingredients on hand as they plate up attractively to form a quick lunch to share with a friend or two. Packed into a picnic hamper, they travel well and are easy to nibble on the wing. Giant platters make excellent grazing food for pre-dinner drinks parties. This form of eating encourages mingling as people become involved with the food. However you go about it, antipasti are an exciting way to share new flavours.

CARAMELISED ONIONS

Caramelised onions are one of the most useful preparations to have on hand in any kitchen. A spoonful added to all kinds of savoury dishes lifts and enhances flavour. Eaten simply, piled onto crusts of bread, their creamy sweetness melts in your mouth.

4 large onions, peeled and sliced

3 tblsp oil

2 tblsp balsamic vinegar

1 tblsp chopped or dried thyme

3 tblsp brown sugar

1 Place all ingredients into a saucepan. Cook very gently for 45 minutes, stirring regularly until caramelised. Cool. Serve as part of an antipasto platter.

Makes 4 cups

Other ideas for an antipasto platter include:

Smoked salmon

Artichoke hearts

Sundried tomatoes

Roasted peppers

Salami or other spicy sausages

Marinated mushrooms

Chargrilled vegetables

ROASTED ASPARAGUS

It may seem surprising to roast a green vegetable but just about any vegetable can benefit from this method of cooking. The nutty flavour which results from roasting asparagus in garlic oil cannot be equalled.

500 g fresh asparagus

1-2 tblsp olive oil

4 cloves garlic, peeled and crushed

salt and pepper

1　Preheat oven to 190°C. Snap or trim ends from asparagus, toss in combined olive oil and crushed garlic. Place into an oven pan, sprinkle with salt. Roast for about 10 minutes until golden. Toss once to allow even cooking.

2　Serve hot or cold as a nibble, as part of an antipasto platter or as a vegetable or salad.

Serves 6

PICKLED VEGETABLES

You can use a different selection of vegetables if you prefer. The pickled vegetables which are layered in jars are very attractive but tend to be for display purposes only. If not pickled correctly, they should not be eaten, especially after an extended period of time.

2 cups white wine vinegar

1 cup water

½ cup sugar

½ tsp turmeric

2 tsp pickling spices

2 bay leaves

2 tsp salt

1 cup cauliflower florets

1 large carrot, peeled and cut into sticks

1 yellow pepper, deseeded

1 red pepper, deseeded

1　Place vinegar, water, sugar, spices, bay leaves and salt into a saucepan. Bring to the boil, stirring until sugar dissolves. Add prepared vegetables, cook for 2 minutes. Remove to a container, cool vegetables in liquid. Store in the refrigerator.

2　Serves as part of an antipasto platter.

Serves 6-8

MARINATED AUBERGINE RIBBONS

Marinating the aubergine raw is unusual but it works to produce a most extraordinary, almost meaty, texture. These aubergine ribbons are a pure taste of Italy.

2 medium aubergines (approx 500 g), trimmed and peeled

coarse salt

¼ cup wine or sherry vinegar

small bunch fresh basil leaves

4 cloves garlic, peeled and sliced

¼ cup capers, drained

extra virgin olive oil

1   Slice aubergines in half lengthways then into long thin ribbons ½ cm thick. Place ribbons into a colander, sprinkle well with salt, toss and leave to drain for 24 hours at room temperature.

2   Next day remove excess moisture by pressing between paper towels. Place in a non-metallic bowl, sprinkle with vinegar, rest for 1 hour.

3   Sterilise a jar large enough to hold the aubergine. Layer ribbons in jar, evenly dispersing basil leaves, garlic and capers throughout. Press down with the back of a spoon. Pour over enough olive oil to cover generously. Seal and refrigerate. Leave for at least one week before eating for flavours to develop. Keeps for up to 6 months in the refrigerator.

Makes about 2 cups

SEMI-DRIED TOMATOES

Partial drying serves to concentrate the flavour intensity of tomatoes, making them tangy, yet sweet and moist at the same time.

olive oil

6-8 ripe tomatoes

salt and pepper

1 Preheat oven to 140°C. Lightly oil an oven tray. Cut tomatoes in half and place face side down on paper towel to drain for about 30 minutes. Turn over and place onto prepared oven tray, sprinkle with salt and pepper. Bake for 1½-2 hours until shrivelled and semi-dried.

2 Serve as a nibble or as part of an antipasto or salad platter.

Serves 6

MARINATED OLIVES

Marinating adds a curious piquancy and flavour to olives.

1 cup Kalamata olives

1 cup green olives or small
   olives for contrast

zest of 2 lemons

3 cloves garlic, peeled and
   sliced

1 tblsp chopped fresh oregano

2 bay leaves

sprigs of fresh thyme

2 red chillies, deseeded and
   sliced

1 tsp toasted fennel seeds

1 cup extra virgin olive oil,
   approximately

1 Drain and dry olives. Make a slit in each olive to help infusion of flavours. Toss through all the other ingredients, cover with olive oil. Cover with plastic wrap and allow to marinate for 24 hours at room temperature. Store in the refrigerator, use within a month.

2 Drain from excess oil to serve. The flavoured oil can be used in a dressing.

Makes about 2½ cups

PARTIAL DRYING SERVES TO CONCENTRATE THE FLAVOUR INTENSITY OF TOMATOES, MAKING THEM TANGY, YET SWEET AND MOIST AT THE SAME TIME

Semi-dried Tomatoes, Marinated Aubergine Ribbons, Marinated Olives and White Beans with Tomato, Garlic and Herbs

ESSENTIALLY CAPERBERRIES HAVE
THE SAME FLAVOUR AS CAPERS BUT
A MORE CRUNCHY TEXTURE, DUE TO
THE SEEDS THEY CONTAIN

Roasted Caperberries in Bacon

WHITE BEANS WITH TOMATO, GARLIC AND HERBS

A dish such as this is a great addition to a mixed antipasto platter but it also makes the perfect small first course. Top with shavings of fresh parmesan and serve with some crusty Italian-style bread such as ciabatta to mop up the juices.

1 cup dried lima, Italian fagiole or white haricot beans

2 bay leaves

1 tblsp wine or sherry vinegar

1 tblsp extra virgin olive oil

2 tblsp sundried tomato dip (see page 23)

2 tomatoes, peeled, deseeded and finely diced

¼ cup gherkins, finely diced

2 tblsp chopped mint

1. Cover dried beans with plenty of cold water and leave to soak overnight.

2. Next day drain beans and place in a large saucepan with fresh water and bay leaves. Bring to the boil then simmer for about 45 minutes or until tender. Drain and while still warm toss with remaining ingredients to dress. Season to taste.

Makes 2 cups

ROASTED CAPERBERRIES IN BACON

Caperberries are the seedpods from the same Mediterranean shrub from which capers are the flowers. Preserved in brine or cured in salt they can be found in all good delicatessens. Essentially caperberries have the same flavour as capers but a more crunchy texture, due to the seeds they contain. The extra bonus is that they come with a nifty built-in cocktail stick – their stalks make them easy to serve and eat as finger food.

4-6 rashers rindless bacon

12 large caperberries, drained and dried

1. Preheat oven to 180°C. Stretch bacon, wrap lengths around each caperberry (one slice of bacon should be enough to cover 3-4 caperberries). Place onto a roasting tray and roast for 10 minutes until bacon is crispy.

2. Drain briefly on paper towel. Serve hot as finger food.

Makes 1 dozen

2 DIPS

Dips are flavourful preparations that are extremely simple to make at home and are used as their name implies – to 'dip' into. Try dipping crackers, fresh bread, crostini (crunchy oven-dried slices of bread brushed with a little oil), fresh or roasted vegetables. All kinds of things can be turned into a purée and called a dip. What I like about dips is their remarkable versatility. In the café kitchen their use can be greatly expanded beyond just dipping and spreading. Thin down a pesto to form a salad dressing, dollop it onto a quickly cooked main course to add colour and flavour, toss it through pasta, blend it into a stuffing or use it as a marinade.

PARSLEY PESTO

Parsley pesto I think is superior to basil in many ways – it is less rich and does not discolour like basil, retaining a dramatic, vivid green. The addition of lemon juice is most refreshing.

1 cup parsley leaves, tightly packed

½ cup lemon juice

1 cup pinenuts, or any preferred nut

1½ tsp salt

½ cup olive oil

1   Place parsley and lemon juice into the bowl of a food processor, process to chop.

2   Add pinenuts and salt, process until well blended. With the motor running drizzle in olive oil to form a smooth paste.

Makes 1¼ cups

WHITE BEAN and GARLIC PURÉE

Purée this dip well to obtain a buttery and almost fluffy texture which combined with the kick of garlic is sensational.

1 cup dried white beans

8 cloves garlic, peeled

1 tblsp chopped parsley

1 tsp salt

¼ cup extra virgin olive oil

1   Soak white beans overnight in plenty of cold water.

2   Next day drain beans and place into a saucepan with fresh cold water. Bring to the boil then simmer gently for about 50 minutes or until beans are very tender, drain well and cool.

3   Place garlic into the bowl of a food processor, pulse to chop. Add parsley, salt and white beans, process to purée. Drizzle in oil to form a smooth paste. Adjust seasoning if necessary.

Makes 2 cups

Parsley Pesto, White Bean and Garlic Purée and Red Pepper and Chilli Dip

RED PEPPER and CHILLI DIP

A most popular café concoction of sweet peppers, creamy nuts with the added bite of chilli.

3 red peppers, halved and deseeded

¼ cup olive oil

¼ tsp chilli powder

1 tblsp wine vinegar

1 cup blanched almonds, or any preferred nut

1 tsp salt

1   Preheat oven to 200°C. Lightly rub pepper halves with oil and place in a roasting pan. Roast for 20 minutes or until skins blister. Remove from oven and cover pan or place pepper into a plastic bag to sweat. This makes the skins easier to remove. Peel off skins and discard.

2   Place pepper flesh, oil, chilli, vinegar and salt into the bowl of a food processor, process to combine. Add almonds and process until smooth – this can take a little time. Adjust seasoning if necessary.

3   Store in the refrigerator. Lasts about one week.

Makes about 2 cups

ARTICHOKE CREAM

A very delicately flavoured purée, as artichokes are themselves naturally quite mild. A spoonful on top of seared or hot smoked salmon is to die for.

1 cup artichoke hearts, drained

2 cloves garlic, peeled

2 tblsp chopped parsley

2 tblsp extra virgin olive oil

1 tblsp lemon juice

½ cup sour cream

salt and pepper

1   Place artichokes, garlic and parsley into the bowl of a food processor, process to purée. Add oil, lemon juice and sour cream, pulse to mix. Adjust seasoning with salt and pepper to taste. Serve as a dip or a sauce with, for example, seared salmon.

Makes about 1½ cups

SPANISH PUMPKIN SEED DIP

An autumnal-coloured and earthy-flavoured dip.

1 cup pumpkin seeds

1-2 fresh chillies, deseeded and
   diced, to taste

2 cloves garlic, peeled

2 tblsp chopped fresh coriander

½ tsp ground cumin

juice of one lemon

2 tblsp tomato paste

¼ cup tomato purée

¼ cup olive oil

salt and pepper

1   Toast pumpkin seeds in an oven preheated to
180°C for 15 minutes. Allow to cool.

2   Place pumpkin seeds, chilli and garlic into the
bowl of a food processor, process to grind.
Add remaining ingredients and process until
mixture is smoothish. Check and adjust
seasoning if necessary.

Makes about 1½ cups

ROCKET PESTO

Rocket is a vivid green, peppery-flavoured herb. Often used as a salad green, it
can also be cooked and has the most outrageous flavour in pesto.

4 cloves garlic, peeled

1 cup rocket leaves, tightly
   packed

1 tsp salt

¼ cup pinenuts

¼ cup grated parmesan

¼ cup extra virgin olive oil

1   Place garlic and rocket leaves into the bowl of a
food processor, pulse well to chop. Add salt, pinenuts
and parmesan, process well to combine. With
motor running drizzle in oil to form a smooth paste.

Makes about 1 cup

OLIVE TAPENADE IS A GREAT FRENCH
PASTE FROM PROVENCE, ESSENTIALLY
MADE OF OLIVES, CAPERS AND ANCHOVIES

Spanish Pumpkin Seed, Olive Tapenade and Sundried Tomato Dip

SUNDRIED TOMATO DIP

I tend to use 'dry' sundried tomatoes, not the ones already in oil. Either are fine but must be softened first so that they can be easily processed into a paste.

1 cup sundried tomatoes

¼ cup balsamic vinegar

¼ cup parsley leaves, tightly packed

3 cloves garlic

¼ cup olive oil

2 tsp sugar

1 tsp salt

½ tsp black pepper

1 Soak sundried tomatoes in balsamic vinegar overnight to soften.

2 Place parsley and garlic into the bowl of a food processor, pulse to chop. Add sundried tomatoes, oil, sugar, salt and pepper. Continue processing until mixture forms a fairly smooth paste. Adjust seasoning to taste.

Makes about 1½ cups

OLIVE TAPENADE

If anchovies are not to your liking they can be omitted but are really not objectionable in this already divinely salty purée.

¼ cup parsley leaves, tightly packed

¼ cup capers, drained

4 cloves garlic, peeled

2 cups Kalamata olives, pitted

5-10 anchovies, optional

juice of one lemon

⅓ cup olive oil

½ tsp ground black pepper

1 Place parsley, capers and garlic into the bowl of a food processor, pulse until well chopped. Add olives, anchovies if desired, lemon juice, oil and black pepper, process to form a fairly smooth paste.

Makes 2½ cups

3 SOUPS

Soups were once possibly the least interesting part of a meal. Happily, they are now often thought of as an exciting meal in themselves. An obvious and popular choice from a café menu, soups have the ability to be infinitely varied in texture, taste and presentation. Increasing familiarity with traditions from other countries has supplied rich possibilities for soup-making. I find soup one of the most versatile and delicious of dishes to cook and serve at home or in the café.

CREAMY POTATO SOUP

Especially good served topped with a dollop of rocket pesto to melt into the soup (see page 21).

**1 large onion, peeled and
 chopped**

4 cloves garlic, peeled

1 tblsp extra virgin olive oil

1 tblsp butter

**4 large potatoes (about 1 kg),
 peeled and roughly chopped**

6 cups vegetable stock or water

½ cup cream cheese

salt

white pepper

1 In a large saucepan sweat onion and garlic in oil and butter until softened but not coloured. Add potatoes and stock or water, bring to the boil. Simmer until potatoes are very tender.

2 Purée mixture in a blender or food processor. This may need to be done in several batches. Add a little cream cheese to each batch.

3 Season well to taste with salt and white pepper. Gently reheat to serve hot.

Serves 4

Creamy Potato Soup

SPICY BLACK BEAN SOUP

Deeply rich in colour, flavour and texture. Dress it up with a dash of sour cream as a garnish.

1 cup black beans

2 red onions, peeled and diced

1 stick celery, diced

1 carrot, peeled and diced

olive oil to cook

3 cloves garlic, peeled and crushed

1 tblsp minced ginger

1 tsp ground cumin

1 tblsp ground coriander

1-2 chillies, deseeded and finely chopped

1 cup chicken stock

1 can tomatoes, chopped

1 tblsp brown sugar

juice of one lemon

salt and pepper

3 tblsp chopped fresh coriander or parsley

sour cream to serve if desired

1   Soak the black beans in plenty of cold water overnight. Drain and place into a saucepan with 1 litre fresh cold water. Bring to the boil then simmer for about an hour or until tender. Reserve 1 cup whole drained beans.

2   In a saucepan sweat diced onion, celery and carrot in oil until softened. Add garlic, ginger, cumin, coriander and chilli, and cook for a few more minutes. Pour in chicken stock, canned tomatoes and brown sugar, simmer for 10 minutes. Add beans and their cooking liquid, lemon juice and salt and pepper. Adjust seasoning if necessary. Stir in freshly chopped herbs just before serving. Top with a little sour cream if desired.

3   Purée in a blender or food processor. Return to the saucepan, add reserved whole beans and gently reheat.

Serves 6

BROCCOLI SOUP

The pure essence of broccoli is captured in this rich, smooth and very green soup.

1 large onion, peeled and chopped

4 cloves garlic, peeled and chopped

2 tblsp olive oil

2 tblsp butter

2 large potatoes, peeled and chopped

4 cups vegetable or chicken stock

600 g broccoli, trimmed and roughly chopped

½ cup cream

salt and pepper

1 Sweat onion and garlic in oil and butter until translucent. Add potatoes and stock, bring to the boil then simmer until potatoes are soft. Add broccoli and boil until just tender but still a vibrant green. Purée soup, return to pan adding cream, salt and pepper and extra stock to thin if necessary.

Serves 4

KUMARA and BACON SOUP

The sweetness of kumara combined with salty bacon works exceptionally well in this soup.

2 tblsp olive oil

2 tblsp butter

2 large onions, peeled and diced

6 rashers rindless bacon, diced

4 large kumara (sweet potatoes)

6 cups chicken or vegetable stock

¼ cup sour cream

salt and pepper

snipped chives

1 In a large saucepan sweat onions in oil and butter until softened but not coloured then remove from pan. Add bacon and gently fry until cooked through and a little crispy. Set aside a few tablespoons of the bacon as a garnish.

2 Place onions, bacon, kumara and stock into saucepan and bring to the boil. Simmer gently until kumara is very tender. Add sour cream and season with salt and pepper.

3 Purée in a blender or food processor. Return to pan to heat through. Adjust seasoning if necessary. Serve topped with extra bacon and snipped chives.

Serves 4

ROASTING CONCENTRATES THE TOMATO FLAVOUR AND GIVES AN ALMOST SMOKY CHARACTER TO THIS SOUP

Roasted Tomato and Lentil Soup

ROASTED TOMATO and LENTIL SOUP

Roasting concentrates the tomato flavour and gives an almost smoky character to this soup. Serve in big bowls with crusty Italian ciabatta bread.

20 ripe tomatoes

1 red onion, peeled and sliced

3 cloves garlic, peeled and crushed

2 tblsp caster sugar

⅓ cup olive oil

¾ cup green or brown lentils

2 litres stock or water

1 bay leaf

1 tsp smoked paprika

2 tblsp tomato paste

½ cup tomato purée

salt and pepper

1 Preheat oven to 200°C. Roughly chop tomatoes. Place onions, garlic, sugar and tomatoes in a roasting pan, drizzle with olive oil. Roast for 45 minutes, tossing occasionally.

2 Meanwhile place lentils, stock or water and bay leaf into a large saucepan. Boil for 45 minutes until lentils are tender. When tomatoes and onions are cooked, tip into lentil pot along with paprika, tomato paste and purée. Mix together and heat through. Adjust seasoning to taste.

Serves 6

CABBAGE SOUP with BLUE CHEESE

Often much maligned, cabbage soup is not bitter and should never be thought ill of. Try this version and be converted. The blue cheese should be of the creamy variety and adds another dimension to the soup. It can be left out, but even non-lovers of blue cheese have been known to take kindly to this combination.

2 large onions, peeled and chopped

2 tblsp olive oil

2 tblsp butter

1 large potato, peeled and chopped

3 cups chicken or vegetable stock

1 good-sized cabbage, thickly sliced

¼ cup cream

½ tsp grated nutmeg

200 g blue cheese (blue brie style)

salt and pepper

1 In a large saucepan sweat onions in oil and butter until soft but not coloured. Add potato and stock, bring to the boil and cook until potato is tender. Add sliced cabbage, boil for 3-4 minutes until cooked but still very green. Add cream, nutmeg and blue cheese.

2 Purée mixture in a blender or food processor until smooth. Gently reheat. Season with salt and pepper to taste.

Serves 6

SWEETCORN CHOWDER

Chowder is generally described as a thick soup containing clams or fish. This is a vegetable version with sweetcorn as its base, but fish could easily be added if desired. Add fish or shellfish at the end so that it cooks briefly and remains tender and juicy.

1 large onion, peeled and finely diced

2 tblsp olive oil

3 large potatoes, diced to 1 cm cubes

2 sticks celery, finely diced

1 red pepper, deseeded and finely diced

1 cup vegetable or chicken stock

2 cups milk

1 450 g can corn kernels

1 450 g can cream style corn

3 spring onions, finely sliced

3 tblsp chopped fresh coriander or parsley

salt and pepper

1 In a large saucepan, sweat onion in oil until softened but not coloured. Add remaining ingredients, except coriander and seasoning. Bring to the boil then simmer until potatoes are cooked through.

2 Purée about ⅓ mixture in a blender or food processor to add body to the soup. Adjust seasoning with salt and pepper to taste and gently reheat. Stir through freshly chopped herbs just before serving.

Serves 6

SPANISH ONION SOUP

Tasted on a journey to Andalucia in the south of Spain, this soup is thickened with bread giving it a velvety consistency.

2-3 cups vegetable or chicken stock

4 slices stale white bread, crusts removed

1 recipe caramelised onion (see page 11)

salt and pepper

1 Pour 1 cup stock over bread and allow to swell.

2 Purée caramelised onion and stock-soaked bread together until smooth, place into a saucepan to gently heat through. If soup is too thick add a little more stock. Adjust seasoning to taste with salt and pepper. Serve hot.

Serves 6

THIS IS A VEGETABLE VERSION WITH
SWEETCORN AS ITS BASE, BUT FISH
COULD EASILY BE ADDED IF DESIRED

Sweetcorn Chowder

PORCINI (SPECIAL ITALIAN DRIED
MUSHROOMS) ARE WORTH FORAGING
FOR IN ANY GOOD DELICATESSEN

Mixed Mushroom and Herb Soup

MIXED MUSHROOM and HERB SOUP

Dark and mysterious, the pungent earthy aroma of porcini permeates this soup.
If you cannot find porcini (special Italian dried mushrooms) the soup will still be
flavoursome but porcini are worth foraging for in any good delicatessen.

15 g dried porcini mushrooms

500 g field mushrooms

**250 g button mushrooms,
    sliced**

**1 large onion, peeled and finely
    diced**

**4 cloves garlic, peeled and
    crushed**

1 tblsp extra virgin olive oil

**2 cups chicken, beef or
    vegetable stock**

1 bay leaf

**1 tblsp each chopped thyme,
    parsley and oregano**

1 tblsp cornflour

salt and pepper

1 Soak the porcini in 2 cups hot water for one
   hour. Purée half the field mushrooms in a food
   processor and thinly slice the remaining
   mushrooms.

2 In a large saucepan sweat the onion and garlic
   in the oil until softened but not coloured. Add
   the mushroom purée, cook until it releases
   water and this evaporates. Add porcini and
   soaking liquid, stock, and bay leaf. Simmer for
   5 minutes then add sliced mushrooms and
   herbs. Mix cornflour with a little water until
   smooth, add to soup and simmer gently for
   5 minutes to thicken. Adjust seasoning with
   salt and pepper to taste.

Serves 4

4 BREADS AND PASTRIES

There is nothing more enticing than the warm yeasty aroma of freshly home-baked bread. Take time to enjoy the bread-making process for it can be most satisfying and the results of your labour even more so. More and more cafés are making their own bread or at least buying in artisan-style breads. This is a trend which needs to be encouraged as it gives variety to both the chef and the customers. We should not settle for anything less than really good bread.

BLUE CHEESE and CARAMELISED ONION LOAVES

The combination of sweet onions and the tart tang of blue cheese are totally engaging.

olive oil

1 recipe multi-purpose bread dough (see page 36)

Filling:

8 tblsp caramelised onions (see page 11)

100 g blue cheese

Topping:

olive oil

sea salt

1 Spray 8 mini loaf tins or large muffin tins with olive oil.

2 Cut dough into 8 equal portions. Flatten each piece of dough into a circle. Place 1 tablespoonful of caramelised onion and a small wedge of blue cheese onto the centre of each disc of dough. Bring all the edges of the dough together, covering the filling. Place each bundle into prepared tins. Leave to rise for 30 minutes.

3 Preheat oven to 210°C. Drizzle loaves with olive oil and sprinkle with sea salt. Bake for 15 minutes or until golden brown and firm.

Makes 8

Blue Cheese and Caramelised
Onion Loaves

MULTI-PURPOSE BREAD DOUGH

A very useful dough for individual bread rolls or something more exotic.

Sponge:

1 tsp sugar

1 tblsp active dry yeast

1 cup warm water

1 cup flour

Dough:

½ cup dry white wine

⅓ cup olive oil

sponge mixture above

2½ cups flour

2 tsp salt

extra flour

1 To make the sponge: sprinkle sugar and then yeast over warm water in a large bowl and leave to activate. Once mixture is frothy (takes 5-10 minutes) add flour and beat until smooth. Cover with cling film, allow to rise for about 30 minutes until mixture bubbles.

2 To make the dough: add wine and olive oil to the sponge. Whisk in flour and salt. Knead dough for 5-10 minutes adding only a little extra flour if necessary. Dough should be very soft and shiny. Place into an oiled bowl, cover with plastic wrap and allow to rise in a warm place for 1 hour or until doubled in volume.

3 Preheat oven to 200°C. Knock back dough and knead briefly. Use as recipe directs.

Makes either:

1 large stuffed bread (calzone)

8 blue cheese and caramelised onion loaves

1 large herb and olive flat bread

STUFFED BREAD (CALZONE)

A single large stuffed bread slices attractively to expose its filling, but individual serving-sized calzone also work well.

olive oil

1 recipe multi-purpose bread
  dough (see page 36)

Filling:

½ cup rocket pesto (see page 21)

4 roasted red peppers

6 semi-dried tomatoes

½ cup blanched spinach

1 cup ricotta

freshly ground black pepper

olive oil

¼ cup parmesan

sea salt

1 Preheat oven to 200°C. Lightly oil a baking tray. Roll prepared dough into a large circle. Place filling ingredients to one side of dough, fold other side over to cover filling. Press edges together and crimp or plait to secure. Leave to rise for 30 minutes. Brush surface with olive oil and scatter with sea salt and parmesan. Bake for 20-25 minutes or until golden brown and firm. This recipe can be used to make smaller individual calzone. Divide the dough and filling evenly between 8 parcels. Bake for 15-20 minutes.

Makes 1 large or 8 small calzone

HERB and OLIVE FLAT BREAD

Great to serve cut into warm shards with a favourite dip or two (see Chapter 2).

olive oil

1 recipe multi-purpose bread
  dough (see page 36)

½ cup Kalamata olives, pitted
  and chopped

2 tblsp chopped fresh herbs:
  thyme, sage, basil (rosemary
  is particularly good)

extra olive oil

extra herbs

sea salt

1 Preheat oven to 200°C. Lightly oil a baking tray.

2 Prepare 1 recipe multi-purpose bread dough but make the additions of chopped olives and herbs when adding the wine and oil. Continue with recipe as usual.

3 Knock back dough and flatten onto prepared baking tray. Drizzle with extra olive oil and scatter with chopped herbs and sea salt. Bake for 30 minutes until crust is golden brown.

Serves 6-8

PANINI ARE THE PERFECT LUNCH – MANY
PEOPLE TAKE THEM AWAY TO TOAST AT
HOME IN THEIR OWN PRESS, GRILL, PAN
OR EVEN TOASTED-SANDWICH MACHINE

Garnet Road Panini – Pastrami and Sundried Tomato (behind)
and Red Pepper and Feta

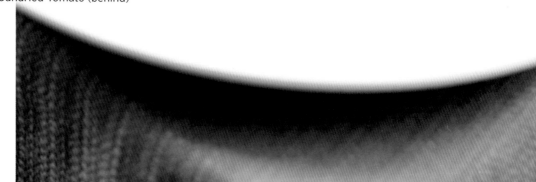

GARNET ROAD PANINI – PASTRAMI and SUNDRIED TOMATO

Panini simply translated means little breads but in New Zealand café culture they have become an icon. They are a little like an upmarket toasted sandwich with exotic fillings. These are our favourites.

4 panini (available from specialist bakeries, or substitute a bap-like bread)

8 tblsp sundried tomato dip (see page 23)

mayonnaise (see whitebait fritters, page 70)

8 large slices pastrami

4 tomatoes, sliced

8 slices mozzarella, edam or creamy havarti cheese

fresh rocket leaves

1   Preheat a panini press, hotplate, grill or even a frying pan. Slice panini in half, spread one side with sundried tomato dip, the other with mayonnaise. Layer pastrami, tomato, cheese and rocket, top with panini half. Toast in press, pan or grill. Serve immediately.

Makes 4

GARNET ROAD PANINI – RED PEPPER and FETA

Strong flavours combine in this meatless version. Panini are the perfect lunch – many people take them away to toast at home in their own press, grill, pan or even toasted-sandwich machine.

4 panini (available from specialist bakeries, or substitute a bap-like bread)

8 tblsp red pepper and chilli dip (see page 20)

mayonnaise (see whitebait fritters, page 70)

200 g feta, crumbled

4 tomatoes, sliced

fresh basil leaves

4 tsp chutney of your choice (see Chapter 10)

1   Preheat a panini press, hot plate, grill or even a frying pan.

2   Slice panini in half, spread one side with red pepper dip, the other with mayonnaise. Sprinkle crumbled feta onto dip, layer with sliced tomato and basil leaves, top with a teaspoonful of chutney and panini half. Toast in press, pan or grill. Serve immediately.

Makes 4

FRENCH ONION TARTS

Top with a dollop of parsley pesto – you will find this the perfect addition to these irresistible tarts.

**1 recipe caramelised onions
(see page 11)**

Paprika pastry:
2 cups plain flour
½ tsp salt
½ tsp smoked paprika
175 g butter
½ cup sour cream

1   Pulse flour, salt and paprika in food processor to sift. Add butter, process until crumbly then mix in sour cream to form a dough. Lightly knead, then chill for 20 minutes. Roll out pastry to 3 mm thick and line eight 12 cm tartlet tins. Chill well. Preheat oven to 200ºC.

2   Fill pastry cases with onions – they will take ½ cupful each. Bake for 25 minutes or until pastry is crisp and onions golden brown.
Makes 8

FETA AND OLIVE LOAVES

Salty flavours of the Mediterranean meld into a muffin-like mixture.

2 cups self-raising flour
1 tsp baking powder
¼ tsp chilli powder
¼ cup grated parmesan
½ cup feta cheese, crumbled
**½ cup stuffed olives, roughly
chopped**
2 tblsp chopped oregano
**1 small onion, peeled and finely
diced**
½ tsp salt
1 egg, beaten
¼ cup oil
1½-2 cups milk

1   Preheat oven to 180ºC. Spray small loaf tins or muffin tins with non-stick spray.

2   Sift flour and baking powder into a large bowl. Add chilli, parmesan, feta, olives, oregano, onion and salt. Make a well in the centre and pour in egg, oil and enough milk to form a smooth batter. Do not over-stir or batter will become tough.

3   Fill tins to just over ½ full. Bake for 25 minutes or until firm and golden brown.
Makes 8 loaves

French Onion Tarts

LUIGI'S MAMA'S PIZZA

My cousin Patty lives in Northern Italy with her husband Luigi and their three beautiful children. Patty is an excellent cook and I have always enjoyed learning from her. She has a great repertoire of authentic Italian recipes, many taught to her by Luigi's Mama. This pizza is easy to serve in the café, cut into wedges as is often the case in pizza-to-go street food stalls in Italy.

Pizza base:

1½ cup warm water

1 tsp sugar

2 tblsp active dried yeast

4 cups plain flour

1½ tsp salt

1½ tblsp olive oil

Pizza topping:

1 cup fresh tomato sauce

2 courgettes, trimmed and sliced

¼ cup shaved parmesan

½ cup olives

¼ cup capers

3 tblsp chopped fresh herbs

salt and pepper

1 Pour warm water into a small bowl, sprinkle with sugar and then yeast. Leave to activate for 5-10 minutes until frothy.

2 Place flour and salt into a large bowl, make a well in the centre. Pour in oil and activated yeast mixture. Mix together into a firm dough. Knead for 5 minutes. Place dough into a lightly oiled bowl and cover with plastic wrap. Leave to rise in a warm place until doubled in volume – this takes about 30-40 minutes.

3 Knock back the dough and lightly knead again. Roll or press out onto a lightly oiled baking tray.

4 Preheat oven to 200°C. Cover with topping ingredients. Bake for 20 minutes or until crust is golden and firm.

Makes 1 large pizza with a thickish base or 2 thin-based pizzas.

PISSALADIÈRE

Caramelised onions again, this time as a stunning pizza alternative.

1 recipe Luigi's Mama's pizza
  base (see page 42)
1 recipe caramelised onions
  (see page 11)
½ cup anchovies
½ cup olives
salt and pepper

1 Preheat oven to 200°C. Roll or press out pizza dough onto a lightly oiled baking tray as in previous recipe instructions.

2 Spread caramelised onions evenly over base. Scatter or lattice-pattern anchovies and olives over onions. Sprinkle with salt and pepper to season. Bake for 20 minutes until crust is firm and golden.

**Makes 1 large thick-based pissaladière or
2 thin-based ones**

BRIOCHE

Brioches are honestly not as hard to make as most people imagine, although the glorious result is certainly worth any amount of effort. They are perfect café breakfast fare served with lemon curd or any fruity jam. Left-over brioches can be substituted for the ordinary bread in the vanilla and apricot bread and butter pudding cake (see page 120). This gives an even more luscious texture to this dessert and nothing goes to waste.

2 tblsp sugar
2 tsp dried yeast
¼ cup warm water
4 cups plain flour
1 tsp salt
1 cup milk, warmed
2 eggs and 2 extra yolks
150 g butter, softened
extra egg for glaze

1 Sprinkle sugar and then yeast onto warm water, leave 5 minutes to activate.

2 Combine flour and salt in a bowl. Add yeast mix, milk, eggs and yolks. Mix well, then work in softened butter. Knead until smooth and glossy.

3 Cover with plastic wrap and leave to rise in a warm place until doubled in volume. This takes about 1 hour.

4 Knock back dough and knead slightly. Shape into 12 even-sized balls, saving some dough. Place into oiled brioche moulds. Shape extra dough into tiny balls and press one into the top of each brioche. Allow to rise for 20 minutes. Preheat oven to 190°C.

5 Glaze with beaten egg. Bake for 15 minutes or until golden brown and firm.

Makes 12

5 SALADS

Salads are the mainstay of café-style food. Think of the classics such as Caesar, Greek and Niçoise, and then let your mind go wild. At the Garnet Road Foodstore I specialise in unusual salad combinations and my salad ideas continue to evolve over time. Salads are where the seasonal changes in produce are visibly revealed, from a mass of aubergines, peppers and tomatoes in the summer to every conceivable root vegetable in the winter. Vegetables we might once never have dreamed of serving cold are now easily tossed into the salad bowl causing further exciting combinations to emerge. Almost anything can be fried, roasted, boiled or steamed then dressed to form a salad. And as for dressings from the café kitchen, anything goes. Take a few basic preparations such as vinaigrette, mayonnaise or salsa, add variations of flavour, colour and texture, and a never-ending supply of interesting dressings is yours. Mix and match dressings and salads as I do at the café to extend the range of salads in this chapter. This is the essence of café-style cooking.

JADE UDON NOODLE SALAD

Hot or cold this is simply delicious. For variety, add vegetables of your choice.

300 g fresh udon noodles

Jade dressing:
½ **cup coriander leaves, tightly packed**
½ **cup parsley**
5 spring onions, roughly chopped
3 tblsp peanut oil
1 tblsp sesame oil
2 tblsp fish sauce
1 tsp soya sauce
1 cup coconut cream

1   Cook udon noodles in boiling water for 3-4 minutes or according to packet instructions. Drain and cool.

2   Place herbs into the bowl of a food processor and pulse to chop. Add remaining dressing ingredients and process into a smooth sauce. Pour over noodles and toss well.

Serves 6

Jade Udon Noodle Salad and
Broccoli with Rocket Dressing

DIVINE COLD BUT ALSO QUITE
AMAZING AS A HOT VEGETABLE DISH.
EXTEND THIS SALAD BY TOSSING
THROUGH SOME ATTRACTIVELY
SHAPED PASTA FOR A CHANGE

Roasted Mediterranean Vegetables
with Balsamic Dressing

ROASTED MEDITERRANEAN VEGETABLES with BALSAMIC DRESSING

Divine cold but also quite amazing as a hot vegetable dish. Extend this salad by tossing through some attractively shaped pasta for a change.

2 large aubergines, trimmed and cubed

6 courgettes, trimmed and thickly sliced

6-12 small red peppers

olive oil to roast

small bunch fresh basil leaves

1 cup Kalamata olives

Balsamic vinaigrette:

4 cloves garlic, peeled and crushed

½ tsp salt

½ tsp freshly ground black pepper

1 tsp sugar

¼ cup balsamic vinegar

¼ cup extra virgin olive oil

Makes ½ cup

1 Preheat oven to 180°C. Whisk vinaigrette ingredients together.

2 Lightly toss aubergines, courgettes and peppers in oil. Roast in separate oven dishes as they will take different amounts of time to cook. If the peppers are tiny, roast them whole; if not cut them into desired shape. Courgettes will take about 10 minutes to cook, aubergines 30 minutes and peppers 30-40 minutes, depending on size. Cool before dressing with balsamic vinaigrette.

3 Arrange on serving platter. Scatter with basil leaves and olives.

Serves 6-8

RED CABBAGE SALAD

This quick-cooking method enhances the flavour of cabbage while retaining its crunchy texture and fabulous colour.

½ small red cabbage

½ cup red wine vinegar

3 tblsp sugar

1 tsp salt

1 tsp tobasco sauce

1 red onion, peeled and sliced

¼ cup currants

2 tblsp chopped fresh parsley

1 tblsp chopped fresh tarragon

1 Remove core and slice cabbage into thin strips.

2 Place the vinegar, sugar, salt, tobasco, onion and currants into a saucepan and bring to the boil. Simmer for 10 minutes until onion has softened and liquid reduced. Add cabbage, toss well, turn up the heat and cook briskly to just wilt cabbage. Turn out into a bowl to cool.

3 Toss through freshly chopped herbs just before serving.

Serves 6

ORIENTAL EGG NOODLE SALAD

Asian flavours are a big part of modern café food. Many chefs mix different ethnic flavours together in fusion dishes. Sometimes this type of coalition can go a bit wrong so I prefer to keep Asian flavours fairly pure and separate.

300 g fine Asian egg noodles

2 cups canned whole baby sweetcorn, drained

1 cup canned straw mushrooms, drained

½ cup canned bamboo shoots, drained

½ cup canned water chestnuts, drained

2 tblsp sesame seeds, toasted

4 spring onions, trimmed and finely sliced

Dressing:

2 tsp sambal oelek or 2 fresh chillies (to taste)

½ cup dark soya sauce

1 tblsp sesame oil

1 tblsp peanut oil

1 Cook noodles in boiling water for 2–3 minutes or according to packet instructions. Rinse with cold water to cool and drain well. Add canned vegetables and sesame seeds.

2 Mix dressing ingredients together and toss well through noodle salad. Serve garnished with finely sliced spring onion and sesame seeds.

Serves 4

MARINATED MUSHROOM SALAD with HAZELNUTS

Mushrooms and hazelnuts have strangely similar flavours and unite beautifully in this salad.

⅓ cup hazelnuts, toasted

3 tblsp red wine vinegar

⅓ cup extra virgin olive oil

salt and pepper

500 g button mushrooms, cleaned

½ cup chopped parsley

1 tblsp dill seeds

1 Place the hazelnuts into the bowl of a food processor and pulse to chop. Add vinegar and oil and process to a fairly smooth paste. Season well to taste. Pour hazelnut dressing over mushrooms, add parsley and dill seeds. Toss well and leave to marinate for at least an hour before serving.

Serves 4

MANY CHEFS MIX DIFFERENT ETHNIC
FLAVOURS TOGETHER IN FUSION DISHES.
SOMETIMES THIS TYPE OF COALITION CAN GO
A BIT WRONG SO I PREFER TO KEEP ASIAN
FLAVOURS FAIRLY PURE AND SEPARATE

Oriental Egg Noodle Salad

49

GREEK SALAD

A classic but always a big favourite with café dwellers.

6 ripe tomatoes, cut into pieces

1 telegraph cucumber cut into cubes

2 red peppers, deseeded and cut into pieces

1 red onion, peeled and cut into large dice

300 g feta cheese, cubed

1 cup Kalamata olives

fresh basil leaves

1 Make vinaigrette by whisking together all ingredients, slowly adding oil until amalgamated.

2 Mix all salad ingredients together, add vinaigrette and toss well.

Serves 6

Garlic vinaigrette:

3 cloves garlic, crushed

1 tsp sugar

½ tsp salt

freshly ground black pepper

2 tblsp red wine vinegar

⅓ cup extra virgin olive oil

PENNE SALAD with PARSLEY DRESSING, CAPERS and ARTICHOKES

Of course any shaped pasta can be used in this salad instead of penne.

300 g penne

⅓ cup capers

1 cup artichoke hearts

Parsley dressing:

3 cloves garlic, peeled

1 cup parsley leaves, tightly packed

2 tblsp capers

2 tblsp caper brine

⅓ cup extra virgin olive oil

salt and pepper

1 Cook the pasta in boiling water until just tender, drain, and set aside to cool.

2 Make the dressing by placing garlic and parsley into the bowl of a food processor, pulse to chop well. Add capers and brine, drizzle in oil until combined. Toss pasta in dressing to coat evenly. Mix through capers and artichoke hearts.

Serves 4-6

FETTUCCINE with TOMATOES, OLIVES and RED PEPPER PURÉE

Fettuccine makes a surprisingly different salad base. Try linguine or even spaghetti for a change as they work well too.

300 g fettuccine or linguine

3 red peppers, halved and deseeded

olive oil for roasting

3 cloves garlic, peeled

1 tblsp red wine vinegar

¼ cup olive oil

salt and pepper

1 punnet cherry tomatoes

1 cup small olives

small bunch fresh basil

1 Cook fettuccine or linguine in boiling water until just tender. Drain and set aside to cool.

2 Preheat oven to 180°C. Rub pepper halves with a little oil, place in a roasting pan and roast for 30 minutes until skins begin to blister. Set aside to cool then remove skins.

3 Make dressing by placing roast peppers, garlic, vinegar and oil into the bowl of a food processor. Process to a smooth paste. Season with salt and pepper to taste. Toss pasta in dressing to coat evenly. Mix through cherry tomatoes, olives and basil leaves.

Serves 6

SPICY ROASTED YAMS with FETA and BACON

Spicy caramelised yams are elevated to even greater heights by the salty intensity of feta and bacon.

1 kg yams, trimmed

¼ cup olive oil

3 cloves garlic, peeled

2 tsp sumac - a Middle Eastern spice (optional)

2 tsp paprika

½ tsp chilli powder

½ tsp black pepper

4 slices rindless bacon, diced

100 g feta, crumbled

2 tblsp chopped fresh parsley

finely grated zest of one lemon

1 Preheat oven to 180°C. Slice yams into even-sized pieces, or leave whole if small. Place into a roasting pan. Rub well with oil, crushed garlic and spices. Roast for 20-30 minutes until tender and slightly caramelised. Allow to cool.

2 Cook diced bacon in a frying pan until crisp. Drain well on paper towel.

3 Arrange yams on serving platter and sprinkle with bacon, feta, parsley and lemon zest.

Serves 6

YELLOW BEETROOT ARE WORTH TRYING FOR THEY HAVE A NICE SUBTLE FLAVOUR AND PRETTY COLOUR

Yellow Beetroot with Mustard,
Feta and Mint

YELLOW BEETROOT with MUSTARD, FETA and MINT

Yellow beetroot are fairly new and sometimes hard to obtain. If you can find them they are worth trying for they have a nice subtle flavour and pretty colour. Ordinary beetroot of course work equally well in this salad – in fact they turn the feta a delightful pink, which is fun.

1 kg yellow or purple beetroot

100 g feta

3 tblsp shredded fresh mint

Mustard dressing:

1 tblsp whole grain mustard

½ tsp salt

½ tsp freshly ground black pepper

1 tsp sugar

juice of 2 lemons

⅓ cup extra virgin olive oil

1   Boil the beetroot in plenty of water until tender. This may take up to an hour depending on the size of the beetroot. Allow them to cool then remove their skins and cut into chunks or slices.

2   Whisk the dressing ingredients together to combine. Toss through the beetroot. Arrange on a serving platter and scatter over crumbled feta and shredded mint.

Serves 6–8

CUCUMBER SALAD WITH ANCHOVY AND TOMATO SALSA

Cucumbers can handle this salsa beautifully, but it also works well with many other foods. Try tossing the salsa through steamed cauliflower, beans, potatoes or pasta for a change.

2 telegraph cucumbers, deseeded

Anchovy and tomato salsa:

2 tblsp anchovies in oil

3 tomatoes, skin and seeds removed

2 cloves garlic, finely chopped

3 spring onions, finely chopped

3 tblsp finely chopped parsley

3 tblsp lemon juice

salt and pepper

1   Slice cucumber attractively and arrange on serving platter.

2   Pound or chop anchovies to form a paste. Finely dice tomato flesh and mix with anchovies and remaining ingredients. Season with salt and pepper to taste. Pile salsa on top of cucumber and serve.

Serves 6

PEANUT RICE SALAD

Crunchy, nutty rice is a great addition to a mixed salad plate in the café or at home.

1 cup jasmine rice

1 cup wild rice

2 cups peanuts, roasted

Dressing:

3 cm piece fresh ginger, grated

4 cloves garlic, crushed

4 tblsp soya sauce

2 tblsp peanut oil

1 tblsp sesame oil

1   Cook the jasmine rice in gently boiling water for 10-12 minutes. Drain and allow to cool. Cook the wild rice in gently boiling water for 25 minutes. Drain and allow to cool.

2   Reserve 1 cup peanuts. Grind up 1 cup of peanuts in a food processor to resemble breadcrumbs. Mix dressing ingredients together.

3   Mix rices, ground peanuts and dressing together well. Garnish with reserved roasted peanuts.

Serves 6-8

BEETROOT, CARROT and SESAME SALAD

Valued for its liver-cleansing properties, beetroot is experiencing an enormous comeback on menus all around town. Its colour contrast makes it the perfect food to plate up with other vibrant salads. In this salad the fusion of lemon and sesame oil is most attractive.

500 g beetroot, peeled

1 large carrot, peeled

2 tblsp sesame seeds, toasted

Dressing:

juice and finely grated zest of 2 lemons

2 tblsp toasted sesame oil

½ tsp salt

½ tsp pepper

1 tsp sugar

1   Grate beetroot and carrot together. A food processor is a fuss-free way to do this but a hand grater is absolutely fine.

2   Mix dressing ingredients into grated vegetables, tossing well to amalgamate.

3   Serve sprinkled with toasted sesame seeds.

Serves 4-6

VALUED FOR ITS LIVER-CLEANSING PROPERTIES,
BEETROOT IS EXPERIENCING AN ENORMOUS
COMEBACK ON MENUS ALL AROUND TOWN

Garnet Road Mixed Salad: Peanut Rice,
Carrot Ribbon, Green Bean and Herb,
and Beetroot, Carrot and Sesame Seeds

55

GREEN BEAN and HERB SALAD with SWEET and SOUR DRESSING

Asparagus when in season can easily be substituted for the beans in this fabulous salad. Serve as a side salad or as part of a mixed salad plate. For a touch of café-style presentation, remove the beans' stem ends but leave the pretty pointy ends intact.

500 g green beans, trimmed

¼ cup mint leaves

¼ cup coriander leaves

¼ cup basil leaves

½ cup rocket leaves

Sweet and sour dressing:

½ tsp salt

¼ tsp freshly ground black pepper

1 tblsp sugar

**1 tblsp sherry vinegar or white
    wine vinegar**

1 tblsp lemon-infused olive oil

2 tblsp extra virgin olive oil

2 tblsp chopped fresh mint

1   Cook the beans in boiling water for about 3 minutes so that they are just tender but still retain their green colour. Drain well, refresh in ice-cold water to cool. Drain and toss with herb leaves.

2   Whisk dressing ingredients together well to combine. Toss dressing through salad and serve immediately.

Serves 4

CARROT RIBBON SALAD

The mustard seeds burst when heated and give the carrots a special pungency. This idea is based on Indian vegetable dishes.

500 g carrots, peeled

3 cloves garlic, peeled

¼ cup vegetable oil

1 tblsp black mustard seeds

salt and pepper

1   With a vegetable peeler, strip long ribbons down the length of each carrot. Crush or process the garlic into the oil to make garlic oil.

2   Either fry ribbons in small batches with portions of the garlic oil and mustard seeds, or place all ingredients into a roasting dish and cook in an oven preheated to 160°C for 20 minutes. Toss half way through to ensure even browning.

3   Season with salt and pepper.

Serves 4-6

BABY POTATO SALAD with REMOULADE

Remoulade mixes a wonderful combination of flavours into mayonnaise. Different results can be easily achieved by adding or substituting ingredients – though of course the result can no longer be called remoulade. The flavour possibilities are endless – try adding anchovies, olives or roasted red peppers, for example.

1 kg baby potatoes, washed

sliced gherkins

Remoulade dressing:

2 egg yolks

2 cloves garlic, peeled

2 tblsp lemon juice

salt

300 ml olive oil

½ cup gherkins, sliced

2 tblsp mint, chopped

1 stalk celery, chopped

¼ cup capers, drained

1 Cook potatoes in boiling salted water until tender. Cool under cold running water, drain well. Toss with remoulade dressing to coat. Serve topped with sliced gherkins.

Remoulade dressing

1 Place yolks, garlic, lemon juice and salt into the bowl of a food processor. Process until mixture becomes pale and creamy. With the motor running, slowly drizzle in the oil until amalgamated. Add gherkins, mint, celery and capers, process to combine.

2 Store in the refrigerator. Lasts up to 10 days.

Serves 6

PICKLED PARSNIPS with PAPRIKA ALMONDS

Smoked paprika is essential for its unbelievable pungent smoky flavour. It is imported from Spain and can be found in all good delicatessens. Ordinary paprika will give colour but not the extraordinary flavour of smoked paprika.

4 medium parsnips, peeled and cut into batons

1 tsp smoked paprika

¼ tsp chilli powder

1 tsp fennel seeds

1 tsp coriander seeds

2 tblsp extra virgin olive oil

½ cup white wine vinegar

½ cup sugar

salt and pepper

½ cup slivered almonds

2 tsp olive oil

1 extra tsp smoked paprika

1 Steam or boil parsnips for about 5 minutes until just tender.

2 Gently fry spices in oil for 1 minute. Add vinegar, sugar, salt and pepper, and boil to reduce slightly. Pour this liquid over parsnips and leave to cool, tossing occasionally to allow parsnips to pickle thoroughly.

3 Toss almonds in olive oil and paprika, place into a small oven pan and toast at 175°C for 5-10 minutes. Sprinkle paprika almonds over parsnips and serve as a salad.

Serves 4

THIS IS AN INCREDIBLY PRETTY SALAD FULL OF DELIGHTFUL FLAVOURS

Broad Beans and Pecorino with
Herb and Caper Salad

BROAD BEANS and PECORINO with HERB and CAPER SALAD

This is an incredibly pretty salad full of delightful flavours. Frozen broad beans are excellent to use instead of fresh if the need arises. Run them under hot water to thaw then remove their skins – they need no further cooking.

500 g broad beans, shelled and peeled

200 g pecorino cheese, cut into 1 cm cubes

3 tblsp extra virgin olive oil

3 tblsp balsamic vinegar

salt and pepper

Herb and caper salad:

½ cup Italian parsley leaves

½ cup basil leaves

¼ cup capers, drained

1 red onion, peeled and very finely diced

3 cloves garlic, peeled and chopped

1   Very lightly blanch broad beans in boiling water, cool. Mix with pecorino cubes. Drizzle with oil and balsamic vinegar and season with salt and pepper. Top with herb and caper salad.

Herb and Caper Salad

1   Toss all ingredients together and spoon onto broad bean and pecorino salad.

Serves 6

BROCCOLI with ROCKET DRESSING

Café cooking is full of improvisation; this dressing also works well over cauliflower, green beans or asparagus.

1 kg broccoli, trimmed into florets

Rocket dressing:

4 cloves garlic, peeled

1 cup rocket, tightly packed

1 tsp salt

½ cup extra virgin olive oil

1   Blanch broccoli florets in boiling, salted water for about 5 minutes until just tender. Drain and plunge into ice-cold water to cool and retain vibrant green colour. Drain broccoli well and toss in rocket dressing.

2   To make dressing, place garlic, rocket and salt into the bowl of a food processor and pulse to chop. With the motor running pour in oil slowly to form a smooth dressing.

Serves 4-6

ORZO with SPICE-ROASTED CARROTS, CURRANTS and PINENUTS

Orzo is a small rice-shaped pasta, sometimes known as riso or risone. It has a delightful silken texture and takes on the flavour and colour of any dressing. Any pasta salad in this book can be made with orzo. Look for it in delicatessens or speciality food shops. It is a great favourite at Garnet Road.

1 cup orzo

½ tsp turmeric (for cooking orzo)

4 carrots, peeled

½ tsp turmeric (for roasting carrots)

oil to roast

1 tsp ground cumin

1 tsp ground coriander

1 tsp paprika

½ cup currants

½ cup pinenuts, toasted

3 tblsp chopped fresh coriander

¼ cup extra virgin olive oil

2 tblsp spiced vinegar

salt and pepper

1   Cook orzo in plenty of boiling water with ½ tsp turmeric added, until just tender. Drain and set aside to cool.

2   Preheat oven to 180°C. Cut carrots in half lengthways then slice on the diagonal into 1 cm thick pieces. Place in a roasting pan, drizzle with a little oil, sprinkle with spices and toss to coat evenly. Roast for 30 minutes, remove and allow to cool.

3   Mix orzo, carrots, currants, pinenuts, coriander, oil and vinegar together well. Season to taste with salt and pepper.

Serves 6

ORZO HAS A DELIGHTFUL SILKEN
TEXTURE AND TAKES ON THE FLAVOUR
AND COLOUR OF ANY DRESSING

Orzo with Spice-Roasted Carrots, Currants and Pinenuts

FOR CENTURIES MEDITERRANEAN COOKS HAVE BEEN MAKING VERSIONS OF THIS SALAD

Mediterranean Roasted Bread Salad

MEDITERRANEAN ROASTED BREAD SALAD

For centuries Mediterranean cooks have been making versions of this salad. Toss yesterday's bread, any appropriate vegetables, herbs and an irresistible dressing together, and create your own interpretation of this classic.

½ **loaf stale rustic bread, cubed**

oil to roast

2 red peppers, halved and deseeded

1 large aubergine, cut into 2 cm cubes

5 ripe tomatoes, cut into wedges

½ **cup caperberries or olives, drained**

fresh basil leaves

vinaigrette (see Roasted Mediterranean Vegetable Salad, page 47)

1 Preheat oven to 180°C. Place bread cubes in a pan and drizzle with a little oil. Roast for 10 minutes until golden brown, cool.

2 Place peppers in oven pan. Drizzle with oil, roast for 20 minutes until skins blister, cool. Remove pepper skins and slice flesh into pieces. At the same time, place aubergine into another pan, drizzle with oil and roast for about 25 minutes until tender, cool.

3 Combine bread, peppers, aubergine and tomatoes. Whisk together vinaigrette ingredients, pour over salad and toss together well. Garnish with fresh basil leaves and caperberries or olives.

Serves 4-6

ROAST PUMPKIN and CHICKPEA SALAD with SUNDRIED TOMATO DRESSING

This is probably one of the most popular salads ever served at the Garnet Road Foodstore. The sundried tomato dressing has many uses – it is also great tossed through pasta, potatoes, even fresh tomatoes.

½ medium crown pumpkin, peeled and cut into large cubes

olive oil for roasting

1 cup chickpeas, soaked overnight in water

2 tblsp finely shredded fresh coriander or mint

Dressing:

½ cup sundried tomatoes

¼ cup red wine vinegar

3 cloves garlic

1 tblsp balsamic vinegar

½ cup extra virgin olive oil

1 tsp sugar

salt and pepper

1. Preheat oven to 190°C. Toss pumpkin cubes lightly in a little oil and place into a roasting pan. Roast for 40 minutes or until tender and lightly caramelised. Allow to cool.

2. Drain chickpeas from soaking water and rinse. Place into a large saucepan and cover with fresh water. Boil for 40-50 minutes or until tender. Drain and allow to cool.

3. To make dressing: heat vinegar and sundried tomatoes together; allow tomatoes to soak in hot vinegar to soften. Place all dressing ingredients into the bowl of a food processor, process to combine. Do not over-whiz – the texture should remain a little chunky. Check and adjust seasoning to taste.

4. Toss pumpkin and chickpeas in dressing, place on serving platter and sprinkle with shredded coriander or mint.

Serves 6

PROBABLY ONE OF THE MOST
POPULAR SALADS EVER SERVED AT
THE GARNET ROAD FOODSTORE

Roast Pumpkin and Chickpea Salad
with Sundried Tomato Dressing

65

COUSCOUS, A GREAT CAFÉ STAPLE, IS EASILY INTERCHANGEABLE WITH THE CRACKED WHEAT

Cracked Wheat with Lemon, Spinach, Herbs and Seeds
and Roasted Purple Onions with Dried Sour Cherries

CRACKED WHEAT with LEMON, SPINACH, HERBS and SEEDS

Couscous, a great café staple, is easily interchangeable with the cracked wheat. Follow exactly the same process of preparation.

1½ cups cracked wheat (or couscous)

juice and finely grated zest of 2 lemons

3 tblsp extra virgin olive oil

small bunch spinach, stems removed and shredded

2 stalks celery, finely diced

2 tblsp each finely chopped coriander, mint and parsley

1 tblsp fennel seeds, toasted

⅓ cup sunflower seeds, toasted

⅓ cup pumpkin seeds, toasted

⅓ cup capers, drained

salt and pepper

1　Place cracked wheat into a large bowl. Pour over 1½ cups boiling water, stir well and cover with plastic wrap. Leave to steam for 15 minutes. Wheat will swell and soften. Uncover and fluff up with a fork.

2　Mix wheat together with remaining ingredients and toss well.

Serves 6

ROASTED PURPLE ONIONS with DRIED SOUR CHERRIES

Sweet onions and balsamic vinegar are perfectly offset by the tart, sour aftertaste of these cherries. If you cannot obtain dried sour cherries, currants or even raisins make good substitutes.

1 kg red onions, peeled

2 tblsp olive oil

⅓ cup balsamic vinegar

½ cup dried sour cherries (available from good delis)

¼ cup brown sugar, tightly packed

3 bay leaves

salt and pepper

1　Preheat oven to 180°C.

2　Slice onions attractively into wedges. Toss with oil, place into a roasting pan. Pour over balsamic vinegar and sprinkle with cherries, brown sugar, bay leaves, salt and pepper. Bake for 30-40 minutes, stirring every now and then until caramelised.

3　Serve hot as a vegetable or allow to cool and serve as a salad.

Serves 6-8 as an accompaniment

Seared Salmon with a
Red Pepper Crust

6 FISH

Fish offers a great opportunity to eat a healthy food that also tastes good. Be sure to buy the freshest possible fish and cook it directly. Simplicity is the key to cooking fish well. Fish of the day is often the best choice on a café menu. Cooked simply in a hot pan with a little butter and a touch of something interesting as a light sauce, there is nothing better.

SEARED SALMON with a RED PEPPER CRUST

Try not to overcook delicate salmon – it is best left with a rare centre portion so that it remains succulent.

3 cloves garlic, peeled

pinch chilli powder

3-4 red peppers, charred, skins removed

2 tblsp olive oil

1 cup fresh breadcrumbs

salt and pepper

extra olive oil

1 side fresh salmon with skin on (approx 1 kg)

1 Prepare crust by placing garlic, chilli and peppers into the bowl of a food processor. Purée, adding about 2 tblsp olive oil and enough breadcrumbs to form a firm paste. Season with salt and pepper to taste.

2 Prepare salmon by removing pin bones and cutting into 6 portions.

3 Preheat grill. Heat a non-stick pan, add a little olive oil, sear salmon pieces quickly for 1-2 minutes on each side. Place onto a grill tray and spoon crust over each piece. Place under grill for 3-4 minutes until crust is golden brown. Serve hot or cold.

Serves 6

WHITEBAIT FRITTERS with LEMON MAYONNAISE

Make tiny versions as finger food, medium fritters for lunch, or giant ones if you're a big whitebait fan.

500 g whitebait

3 eggs, lightly beaten

½ cup finely chopped parsley

salt and pepper

oil for frying

Lemon mayonnaise:

2 egg yolks

½ tsp salt

½ tsp mustard

zest and juice of one lemon

½ cup olive oil

½ cup vegetable oil

1 Mix all fritter ingredients together, seasoning well with salt and pepper. Fry large spoonfuls for a couple of minutes on each side. Remove and drain on paper towel. Serve with lemon mayonnaise to dip.

Makes 12 medium fritters

Mayonnaise

1 Place yolks, salt, mustard, zest and juice into the bowl of a food processor. Process until pale and foamy. With the motor running add oil in a thin and steady stream until combined. Add a little extra lemon juice to thin if necessary.

Makes 1½ cups

TUNA ESCABECHE

Tuna transcends flavour boundaries when marinated in this very Spanish way.

1-1.5kg fresh tuna, skin removed

Marinade:

½ cup olive oil

⅓ cup white wine vinegar

⅓ cup water

⅓ cup lemon juice

6 cloves garlic, peeled and finely sliced

pinch cayenne pepper, or hot paprika

½ cup capers, drained

½ cup roasted red peppers, cut into julienne strips

small bunch fresh thyme

3 lemons cut into wedges

1 Slice tuna into 6 even-sized pieces. Heat a frying pan with a little oil, sear tuna for 2-3 minutes on each side to produce medium rare (cook a little longer if your preference is for well done). Place into a deep dish, pour over marinade while still warm. Leave to marinate for at least 24 hours for flavours to develop. Serve garnished with lemon wedges.

Marinade

1 Place all ingredients into pan in which tuna was seared. Bring to the boil then pour over the tuna.

Serves 6

Whitebait Fritters with
Lemon Mayonnaise

SEAFOOD PAELLA

The rice is the most important ingredient in paella. It should be of medium grain and give an authentic consistency to the finished dish that is only slightly creamy and full of flavour. Add chorizo (Spanish sausage) if you can find it or chicken if you desire.

12 mussels, scrubbed

12 raw green prawns, peeled and deveined

12 scallops

200 g white fish fillets, cubed

lemon juice

3 tblsp olive oil

1 red onion, peeled and diced

3 cloves garlic, peeled and crushed

2 cups paella rice

3 cups stock (use reserved poaching liquid, fish or chicken stock)

½ tsp saffron

pinch chilli powder

1-2 tsp smoked paprika

1 bay leaf

1 cup white wine

3 tomatoes, peeled and chopped

salt and pepper

1 In batches, briefly poach all seafood in a small amount of gently simmering water with a dash of lemon juice added. Set aside seafood, strain poaching liquid to use as stock.

2 Heat oil in a large frying pan, add onion and garlic. Cook without browning until soft. Add rice, stir to coat with oil.

3 Heat stock with saffron added to dissolve. Add spices, bay leaf, white wine and tomatoes to the rice. Bring to the boil then simmer for 15-20 minutes uncovered. Season with salt and pepper.

4 Add the seafood, cover and allow 5 minutes to gently steam heat through. The rice should be cooked and the liquid evaporated. Fluff up rice to serve.

Serves 6

Seafood Paella

FRESH TUNA NIÇOISE

Another classic salad, this uses fresh seared tuna instead of canned in a modern café twist. Think of glorious days in Nice or anywhere warm and sultry.

1 kg fresh tuna, skin removed

salt and pepper

oil for frying

300 g thin green beans, blanched and refreshed

500 g baby potatoes, halved and cooked

4-6 tomatoes, cut into wedges

⅓ telegraph cucumber, sliced

6 hard-boiled eggs, quartered

10-15 anchovies

½ cup olives

lemon wedges to serve

Lemon juice dressing:

juice of 2 lemons

⅓ cup extra virgin olive oil

salt and pepper

1   Cut tuna into 6-8 portions and season with salt and pepper. Heat a frying pan, add a little oil and sear tuna for a few minutes on each side depending on thickness of pieces. Tuna pieces need to be rare in the centre as if overcooked tuna becomes very dry.

2   Combine salad ingredients, top with seared tuna, anchovies and olives. Drizzle over lemon juice dressing and serve with lemon wedges.

3   Make dressing by whisking lemon juice and oil together and seasoning with salt and pepper to taste.

Serves 6-8

7 MEAT

We can all easily appreciate high quality meats that need little cooking or adulteration to bring them to perfection. Intriguingly, though, slowly cooked cuts of inexpensive meat are extremely popular once again. In the hands of café chefs even sausages and meatloaf have been turned into something trendy. Today the meat course embraces a whole world of different cooking techniques, new ideas and new ingredients. Cooking interesting meat dishes is simply a matter of intelligently marrying the lot together.

VEAL SALTIMBOCCA

Simply serve these tender veal parcels with the fragrant juices of the pan.

4 veal schnitzels

salt and pepper

½ cup fresh sage leaves

8 tblsp ricotta cheese

4 slices ham

¼ cup shaved parmesan

olive oil for frying

50 g butter

½ cup Marsala or sherry

juice of one lemon

1 Spread out veal, flatten with a mallet to 3 mm thick. Season with salt and pepper. On each piece, lay 2–3 sage leaves in centre. Top with 2 tblsp ricotta, cover with a slice of ham, some parmesan and 2–3 more sage leaves. Wrap up veal to enclose filling. Chill for 30 minutes.

2 Heat oil in frying pan over a moderate heat. Fry parcels for 5 minutes on each side until cooked through. Remove to a warm serving plate. Melt butter in same pan; deglaze with Marsala or sherry. Add a few extra sage leaves and lemon juice. Check seasoning. Pour over veal to serve.

Serves 4

Veal Saltimbocca

Summer Lamb Meatloaf

SUMMER LAMB MEATLOAF

Old-fashioned foods are big on café menus and a good meatloaf is not easy to pass up. Serve hot or cold with a favourite chutney.

1 kg lamb mince

1 medium onion, peeled and chopped

5 cloves garlic, peeled and chopped

2 tblsp olive oil

½ cup tomato paste

150 g rindless bacon, chopped

½ cup fresh breadcrumbs

1 egg

2 tsp salt

2 tsp black pepper

1 tblsp chopped fresh oregano, or other fresh herb

juice and zest of 2 lemons

6 extra slices rindless bacon

1   Preheat oven to 200ºC. Mix all ingredients together (except extra bacon) until well blended. Shape into 2 long loaves. Wrap each loaf in 3 slices of bacon. Place into an oiled oven pan. Bake for 50-60 minutes. Serve hot or cold, cut into slices. Delicious with red pepper and caper relish (see page 99).

Serves 8-10

HERB, SUNDRIED TOMATO and OLIVE-COATED RACK OF LAMB

This is a divine coating for rack of lamb. Get your butcher to trim the lamb racks for ease of preparation. Figure on one rack serving two people unless they have large appetites.

½ cup Italian parsley, chopped

½ cup finely chopped sundried tomatoes

½ cup chopped pitted Kalamata olives

1 tblsp wholegrain mustard

2 racks of lamb, trimmed

salt and pepper

1 egg, beaten

olive oil

1   Preheat oven to 200ºC. Mix parsley, sundried tomatoes, olives and mustard together. Season lamb racks with salt and pepper, dip into beaten egg and then press chopped mixture firmly onto meat. Place into a roasting dish and drizzle with olive oil.

2   Roast for around 15-20 minutes, depending on how pink you like your meat. Allow meat to rest for 10 minutes before slicing into individual ribs, or serve half a rack per person.

Serves 4

MOROCCAN LAMB TAGINE with PRESERVED LEMONS

A very spicy brew full of the flavours of Morocco. The preserved lemons (see page 99) are an authentic accompaniment to a dish such as this.

olive oil

1 kg diced lamb

2 large onions, peeled and finely diced

1 tblsp harissa (recipe below)

½ cup whole garlic cloves, peeled

1 tblsp ground coriander

1 tblsp ground cumin

1 tsp ground turmeric

1 tsp paprika

1 tsp ground cinnamon

1 tsp black mustard seeds

6 cups chicken stock

salt

1 Preheat oven to 180°C. Heat a frying pan, add oil and fry lamb in batches to brown and seal meat. Place lamb into a baking pan.

2 Lower the heat and sweat the onions until softened. Add harissa, garlic cloves and spices and fry briefly. Add stock and bring to the boil. Pour over lamb, cover pan and bake for 1 hour. Remove covering and bake for a further 20 minutes. Check flavour of sauce, adding a little salt if necessary. Serve with thinly sliced preserved lemon peel.

HARISSA

This fiery sauce is a staple of North African cooking. It can be mild or extremely hot depending on the variety of chilli peppers used. Serve extra harissa on the side for those who like more heat. Commercially prepared harissa is often available in speciality food stores.

100 g dried chillies, soaked 5 minutes in warm water

6 cloves garlic

1 tsp salt

2 tblsp olive oil

1 tblsp caraway seeds, toasted

1 tblsp coriander seeds, toasted

1 Drain chillies. Place all ingredients into the bowl of a food processor and process until smooth.

2 Store in the refrigerator, covered with a film of oil. Lasts about 3 months.

Makes 1¾ cups

A VERY SPICY BREW FULL OF THE FLAVOURS OF MOROCCO. THE PRESERVED LEMONS ARE AN AUTHENTIC ACCOMPANIMENT TO A DISH SUCH AS THIS

occan Lamb Tagine with Preserved Lemons

THIS RECIPE PROVES THAT
JUST ABOUT ANYTHING CAN
BECOME CAFÉ-STYLE FOOD

Corned Beef and Kumara Cottage Pie

CORNED BEEF and KUMARA COTTAGE PIE

This recipe proves that just about anything can become café-style food. The buttery sweet-potato and the slightly salty ground corned beef melt together in flavour and texture.

1 onion, finely diced

4 tblsp oil

3 tblsp flour

1 400 g can tomatoes, crushed

500 g corned beef, cooked and diced

3 tblsp chopped fresh parsley

1 kg kumara

100 g butter

salt and pepper

heated cream or milk

grated cheese

1   In a saucepan sweat onion in oil until softened. Stir in flour off the heat. Add tomatoes and blend to a smooth consistency. Cook until thickened, cool. Mince or finely grind corned beef in a food processor. Mix tomatoes, beef and parsley together and place in the base of 6 ovenproof dishes or one large dish.

2   Cook kumara in boiling water until tender, drain and return to the heat, shaking to dry. Mash well or mouli to remove lumps. Add butter, salt and pepper and enough cream or milk to achieve a creamy firm texture. Spoon kumara mash onto corned beef and top with grated cheese.

3   Preheat oven to 180°C. Bake pies for 20 minutes until heated through and cheese is melted and golden brown. Serve with a favourite chutney (see Chapter 10).

Serves 6

BALSAMIC BEEF SALAD

A bit of a play on Thai beef salad, this is an Italian version showing how innovative café cooking can be. Plate up this salad with lots of height to display the subtle colour combinations.

750g eye fillet of beef

Dressing:
⅓ cup balsamic vinegar
½ cup extra virgin olive oil
4 cloves garlic, crushed
2 tsp brown sugar
1 tsp wholegrain mustard
1 tblsp chopped fresh oregano
salt and pepper

Salad:
3 good handfuls mesclun (mixed baby salad leaves)
½ bunch celery, thinly sliced on a sharp angle
1 bunch spring onions, thinly sliced
2 tblsp capers

1 Preheat oven to 220°C. Sear beef very quickly in a hot frying pan to seal. Roast for 20-30 minutes depending on preference for rare meat. Allow to cool then slice thinly.

2 Whisk all the dressing ingredients together and season with salt and pepper to taste. Pour dressing over sliced beef and allow to marinate for at least one hour.

3 Toss salad ingredients, beef and balsamic dressing together well.

Serves 4

LAMB SHANKS AND PARSLEY MASH

A very fashionable item on menus – long, slow, moist cooking is the key to perfect lamb shanks. Try serving the lamb and mash in a bowl to hold the flavoursome juices.

8-10 lamb shanks

oil to fry

1 onion, finely chopped

3 cloves garlic, crushed

2 cups red wine

3 cups beef stock

2 cups canned tomatoes, crushed

4 bay leaves

1 tblsp chopped fresh rosemary

salt and pepper

1 Preheat oven to 170°C. Heat a frying pan, add a little oil and the lamb shanks and cook for 2 minutes on each side or until well browned. Place shanks into a roasting pan.

2 Lower the heat and sweat onion and garlic in same pan. Add red wine, stock and tomatoes and bring to the boil. Pour over lamb, tuck in bay leaves and sprinkle with rosemary, salt and pepper. Cover pan and bake for about 2–2½ hours, turning once, until lamb is very tender. Check seasoning of sauce and serve with parsley mash.

Serves 6

PARSLEY MASH

A modern twist to mash.

1 kg floury potatoes, peeled

100 g butter

¼ cup finely chopped parsley

milk or cream, heated

salt and pepper

1 Cut potatoes into large chunks. Cook in boiling water until tender. Drain potatoes and return to the heat, shaking to dry. Mash or mouli well to remove lumps. Add butter, parsley and enough milk or cream to achieve preferred consistency. Season with salt and pepper.

Serves 6

Mediterranean Chicken

<u>8</u> CHICKEN

Chicken is possibly the most versatile and adaptable of all meats. Its compatibility with many different flavours, seasonings and cooking methods makes it a great favourite both to cook and to eat. Chicken skilfully featured on the café menu is a most popular choice as meal of the day.

MEDITERRANEAN CHICKEN

The perfect chicken dish for a summer's day, combining all the flavours of the Mediterranean.

6 chicken breasts, skin removed

3 tblsp olive oil

2 red onions, peeled and cut into wedges

2 red peppers, deseeded and sliced

2 400 g cans tomatoes, crushed

1 tblsp sugar

2 bay leaves

1 cup stuffed green olives

salt and pepper

½ cup garlic cloves

1 Preheat oven to 180°C. Heat a chargrill or frying pan, add oil and sear chicken breasts to seal. Remove chicken to a roasting pan. Lightly cook onion wedges and pepper slices, and place over chicken. Heat tomatoes and sugar, add bay leaves and olives and season with salt and pepper. Pour sauce over chicken. Bake for 20 minutes.

2 In a separate pan roast whole garlic cloves in a little oil for 10 minutes.

3 Serve each chicken breast with a generous portion of vegetables and sauce and a few roasted garlic cloves.

Serves 6

TAMARIND CHICKEN

Tamarind, the sour pulp of bean-like seedpods of a tropical plant, can be purchased from Asian and speciality food stores. It comes in liquid or compressed block forms. The compressed block needs soaking before use. Soak in hot water and work into a paste, strain and discard seeds.

100 g block tamarind

2 cups boiling water

6 chicken breasts

2 cm piece ginger, grated

3 tblsp palm or brown sugar

3 tblsp soya sauce

2 red peppers, halved and deseeded

300 g whole baby sweetcorn, trimmed

salt and pepper

1 Pour boiling water over tamarind pulp. Mash and work into a paste, strain and discard seeds – this produces tamarind water. Preheat oven to 180°C.

2 Sear chicken breasts in a hot pan to seal, place into a roasting pan. Mix tamarind water, ginger, sugar and soya sauce together and pour over chicken. Slice peppers thickly and add to pan with sweetcorn. Roast for 15 minutes or until just cooked through.

3 Check seasoning and thicken sauce with a little cornflour if desired.

Serves 6

VIETNAMESE CHICKEN SALAD

Crisp vegetables and tender chicken are enhanced with a distinctive sweet and sour dressing.

6 chicken breasts, skins removed

2 carrots, peeled

½ telegraph cucumber

1 cup mung bean sprouts

1 cup mizuna lettuce

½ cup mint leaves

3 tblsp chopped fresh coriander

Vietnamese dressing:

3 tblsp lime juice

2 tblsp fish sauce

2 tblsp rice vinegar

3 tblsp palm or brown sugar

½ cup water

1 chilli, finely chopped

2 cloves garlic, thinly sliced

1 Poach chicken breasts in water or stock for 15 minutes. Refrigerate in cooking liquid until cold. Slice thinly on the diagonal.

2 Cut carrots in half lengthways then finely on the diagonal. Halve cucumber, remove seeds and slice finely.

3 Whisk dressing together until sugar has dissolved. Mix all salad ingredients together, toss well in dressing and serve.

Serves 6

CHICKEN INVOLTINI

Involtini are stuffed savoury parcels, in this case made with chicken. These rustic bundles can be left whole or attractively sliced, and served hot or cold.

1 onion, finely diced

2 cloves garlic, crushed

2 tblsp oil

2 tblsp butter

2 cups fresh breadcrumbs

4 tblsp finely shredded basil

1 red pepper, finely diced

¼ cup pitted olives, finely diced

1 egg, lightly beaten

salt and pepper

16 boneless chicken thighs

8 slices rindless bacon

grated parmesan

salt and pepper

1 Sweat onion and garlic in oil and butter over a low heat until softened. Mix breadcrumbs, onion, garlic, basil, red pepper and olives together to form a stuffing. Season with salt and pepper and bind with beaten egg. Preheat oven to 180°C.

2 Lay out 8 chicken thighs and cover with stuffing mixture, top each with another thigh. Wrap each parcel with a slice of bacon to secure filling. Place in a roasting pan. Sprinkle with parmesan and salt and pepper. Roast for 20 minutes until bacon is crisp and chicken cooked through.

Serves 8

CRISP VEGETABLES AND TENDER CHICKEN ARE ENHANCED
WITH A DISTINCTIVE SWEET AND SOUR DRESSING

Vietnamese Chicken Salad

THIS PAPRIKA PASTRY IS FAIRLY SPEEDY TO PREPARE

Chicken and Broccoli Pie

CHICKEN and BROCCOLI PIE

There are several stages to assembling this pie and although the paprika pastry is fairly speedy to prepare, store-bought pastry is a fine substitute if you are short of time.

Paprika pastry:

3 cups flour

½ tsp salt

½ tsp paprika

250 g butter, cubed

½ cup sour cream

Filling:

5 chicken breasts, skin removed

400 g head of broccoli

125 g butter

3 cloves garlic, crushed

5 tblsp flour

2½ cups stock

¼ cup cream

salt and pepper

1   To make pastry, pulse flour, salt and paprika in a food processor to sift. Add butter, process until crumbly then mix in sour cream to form a dough. Lightly knead, chill for 20 minutes.

2   Poach chicken breasts in a saucepan just covered with gently simmering water for 15 minutes. Strain liquid for stock. Cool chicken and slice.

3   Cut broccoli into florets. Blanch in boiling water for 3 minutes. Drain and plunge into ice-cold water to cool. Drain and dry well.

4   Melt butter in a saucepan, add garlic and flour off the heat and mix to a smooth paste. Add stock, stirring to incorporate. Return to the heat and cook until thickened. Add cream and salt and pepper to taste. Cool.

5   Roll $^2/_3$ pastry to 3 mm thick and line a 24 cm loose-bottom pie tin. Mix chicken and broccoli with sauce and pack into pastry case. Roll out remaining pastry into a circle to cover filling. Fit pastry onto pie and crimp edges to bind. Chill for 20 minutes. Preheat oven to 190°C.

6   Bake for 45 minutes or until pastry is crisp and golden brown.

Serves 8-10

9 GRAINS AND PULSES

Grains and pulses can be combined with other ingredients in almost limitless ways. They act as flavour sponges, soaking up the nuances of the dish in which they are cooked. Also incredibly satisfying in their own right, grains and pulses provide an excellent and inexpensive source of protein. These often under-appreciated healthy staples have enormous culinary potential both for vegetarian and meat meals.

CHICKPEA BURGER

These burgers are not your average vegetarian meal – in truth they are better! The mouth-watering moist patties can be combined with any favourite burger ingredients.

8 burger buns

mayonnaise (see whitebait
    fritters, page 70)

3 tomatoes, sliced

sliced beetroot if desired

lettuce

rocket pesto (see page 21)

red pepper and caper relish (see
    page 99)

Chickpea patties:

1 cup chickpeas, soaked overnight
    in water

1 bay leaf

½ cup peanuts, roasted

2 onions

3 cloves garlic, crushed

2 tblsp oil

pinch cayenne pepper

2 tblsp each chopped parsley
    and basil

2 tsp soya sauce

½ cup fresh breadcrumbs

½ cup flour

1 egg, beaten

salt and pepper

oil for frying

1   Drain chickpeas and rinse. Place in saucepan with fresh water and bay leaf. Bring to the boil then simmer for 40-50 minutes until tender. Drain and cool. Grind in a food processor to resemble breadcrumbs. Grind peanuts.

2   Sweat onion and garlic in oil to soften. Combine burger ingredients and form into 8 patties. If mixture is very sloppy add a little more flour. Fry patties over a moderate heat for 3 minutes on each side.

3   Fill burger buns with desired salad ingredients, condiments and chickpea patties.

Serves 8

Chickpea Burger

BARLEY HAS A RICH CREAMY RISOTTO
TEXTURE WHEN COOKED BY THIS METHOD
AND A GORGEOUS NUTTY FLAVOUR

Barley and Mushroom Risotto

BARLEY and MUSHROOM RISOTTO

A risotto made with barley instead of rice! Barley has a rich creamy risotto texture when cooked by this method and a gorgeous nutty flavour. Serve as a meal in itself or as an accompaniment to meat, chicken or even fish.

1 cup dried mushrooms

3 cups vegetable or chicken stock

1 large onion, finely diced

4 cloves garlic, crushed

1 tblsp olive oil

50 g butter

2 cups pearl barley

1 cup fresh button mushrooms, sliced

1 cup red wine

2 tblsp chopped parsley

salt and pepper

1 Soak dried mushrooms in 2 cups hot water for 20 minutes to soften. Drain and reserve liquid as stock.

2 Heat stock and mushroom water in a saucepan. In a large heavy-based saucepan sweat onion and garlic in oil until softened. Add butter to melt. Add barley and mushrooms, toss to coat in oil and butter and cook for a few minutes. Add red wine, bring to the boil then simmer until wine evaporates.

3 Add a ladleful of hot stock. Each time liquid evaporates add another ladle of stock and continue simmering mixture for 30 minutes, stirring occasionally. Mixture should be sloppy and barley tender.

4 Add parsley and season well to taste. Stir through softened mushrooms, turn off heat, cover and allow to steam for 5 minutes to finish.

Serves 4

COUSCOUS with LAMB and HARISSA

Vegetarian options are very important in today's café menus. Couscous is a great base for vegetables as well as meat. This recipe can easily be altered to create a veritable vegetable feast. Omit the lamb, of course, adding maybe feta, sundried tomatoes and grilled courgettes.

600 g boneless lamb leg steaks

½ cups vegetable or chicken stock

¼ cup olive oil

2 cloves garlic, crushed

1 tsp turmeric

½ tsp ground cinnamon

2 cups instant couscous

**2 red peppers, deseeded, roasted and
  sliced**

½ cup whole almonds, toasted

zest and juice of 2 lemons

3 tblsp chopped fresh mint

salt and pepper

harissa to serve (see page 78)

1 Cook lamb under a preheated grill or in a frying pan for 3-5 minutes on each side, depending on thickness of steaks and preference for pinkness. Cool and slice thinly.

2 In a large saucepan heat chicken stock, oil, crushed garlic, turmeric and cinnamon. Stir in couscous, cover and allow to steam for 5 minutes.

3 Fluff up couscous with a fork, add lamb and remaining prepared ingredients. Season to taste with salt and pepper. Serve with harissa for those who like a hot kick to their meal.

Serves 4

POLENTA

If you've ever had polenta and not enjoyed it, please try my recipe and give polenta one more chance! Not only is it delicious in taste and texture but this method makes polenta production stress-free and leaves you with a clean saucepan, which other versions don't!

4 cups water

4 cloves garlic, peeled and crushed

2 tblsp olive oil

2 tsp salt

1 cup polenta (cornmeal)

100 g butter

½ cup freshly grated parmesan

1   Bring water to the boil, add oil, garlic and salt. Rain in the polenta, stirring constantly, adding butter and parmesan. Cover saucepan, turn off heat and allow to steam for 30-40 minutes to soften.

2   Serve as a savoury porridge or turn out polenta into a dish moistened with water and allow to set. Cut into pieces, grill or fry until crisp and hot. Serve as an accompaniment to meat or vegetable dishes.

Serves 10

LAYERED POLENTA CAKE

The layers in this pretty savoury polenta cake can be varied according to taste or whatever you have on hand. Make a totally vegetarian version layering with different vegetables or a meat rendition with the layers interspersed with meat sauce.

1 recipe polenta (see previous recipe)

100 g prosciutto

1 bunch spinach, blanched and drained on paper towel

200 g gorgonzola or other soft blue cheese

freshly ground black pepper

1   Make polenta (above). Preheat oven to 200°C.

2   Butter a springform cake tin. Spread ⅓ soft polenta mixture in base of tin. Layer half the prosciutto, spinach, then gorgonzola and pepper over polenta. Repeat layers, finishing with polenta. Bake 30 minutes until golden and heated through. Roast a few slices of prosciutto on a baking tray for 5 minutes until crisp.

3   Remove from cake tin and slice into wedges, garnish with roasted prosciutto.

Serves 10

IF YOU'VE EVER HAD POLENTA AND NOT
ENJOYED IT, PLEASE TRY MY RECIPE AND
GIVE POLENTA ONE MORE CHANCE!

Layered Polenta Cake

95

From the top: Tamarillo Chutney,
Rhubarb Chutney and
Cranberry and Mint Chutney

<u>10</u> PRESERVES

Preserves provide enormous variety to cooking and eating. Served in their simplest form with bread or used as accompaniments for both sweet and savoury dishes, nothing matches the full flavour of home-made preserves. The incredible feeling of satisfaction from having prepared your own jam or chutney can only be matched by the joy of eating it.

MY GRANDMOTHER'S TAMARILLO CHUTNEY

My grandmother always made us her special 'tree tomato' chutney. It was my favourite as a child and still is today.

12 tamarillos

2 apples, peeled and diced

2 onions, peeled and diced

2 cups brown sugar

1¼ cups malt vinegar

1 tblsp salt

1 tblsp mixed spice

1 tsp cayenne pepper

1   Plunge tamarillos into boiling water for one minute then cool in cold water. Split skins, remove and discard. Chop flesh and place with remaining ingredients into a large saucepan or preserving pan. Boil gently for about one hour until thick. Ladle into hot sterilised jars and seal well.

Makes about 6 cups

RHUBARB and RAISIN CHUTNEY

A tangy fruit chutney perfect with bread, cheese or meats.

500 g rhubarb, washed and chopped into 1 cm pieces

500 g onions, peeled and diced

1 cup spiced vinegar

3 cups raw sugar

1 tsp ground cinnamon

½ tsp ground cloves

½ tsp chilli powder

1 cup raisins

2 tsp salt

1   Combine all ingredients in a large saucepan or preserving pan. Bring to the boil then simmer until thick and pulpy – this takes about 30-40 minutes. Ladle into hot sterilised jars and seal well.

Makes about 6 cups

CRANBERRY and MINT CHUTNEY

Obviously appropriate for Christmas fare, or all the year round for that matter. Frozen cranberries are readily available.

2 cups wine vinegar

2 cups sugar

3 cm piece fresh ginger, peeled and finely chopped

3 onions, peeled and finely sliced

1 tsp ground cinnamon

1 tsp ground nutmeg

juice and zest of 2 lemons

2 tsp salt

½ tsp cayenne pepper

1 kg cranberries (frozen are fine)

2 tblsp chopped fresh mint

1 Place all ingredients except cranberries and mint into a large saucepan or preserving pan. Bring to the boil then simmer uncovered until slightly syrupy, about 15 minutes. Stir in cranberries and mint. Cook further 5-10 minutes until cranberries burst. Ladle into hot sterilised jars and seal well.

Makes about 6 cups

PICKLED KUMQUATS

Kumquats differ from other citrus fruits in that the skin is sweeter than the flesh. They produce an interesting tart-sweetness which works well with cardamom.

3 cups kumquats, sliced in half

1 tsp salt

1 cup white wine vinegar

½ cup sugar

seeds from 4 cardamom pods, crushed

2 cm piece fresh ginger, peeled and thinly sliced

1 Place the kumquats and salt into a saucepan and cover with water. Bring to the boil then simmer for 5 minutes, drain and discard any pips.

2 Bring vinegar, sugar, cardamom and ginger to the boil, stirring until sugar dissolves. Add kumquats, bring back to the boil. Ladle into hot sterilised jars and seal well. Store in a cool dark place for at least 4 weeks to develop flavours before eating.

Makes about 3 cups

PRESERVED LEMONS

This method of preserving lemons is typical of North African and especially Moroccan cooking. Traditionally only the silken-textured peel of the preserved fruit is used in cooking or as a condiment.

10 whole lemons

10 tblsp salt

juice of 5 lemons

1   Wash lemons well. Divide into quarters, not quite cutting them all the way through. Pack 1 tblsp salt into cuts of each lemon. Press lemons firmly into an appropriately sized sterilised jar. Pour over lemon juice and then enough boiling water to completely cover. Seal well.

2   Store in a cool place, shaking the jar every day for two weeks. Once preserved, store in the refrigerator. Preserved lemons will keep up to six months. Rinse well before using.

RED PEPPER and CAPER RELISH

A sweet chutney with Mediterranean flavours.

1 tblsp olive oil

1 cup preserved julienne red peppers, drained

or 2 fresh red peppers, deseeded and cut into julienne strips

1½ cups canned tomatoes, roughly crushed

½ cup balsamic vinegar

¼ cup red wine vinegar

¾ cup white sugar

¼ tsp ground allspice

1 tsp salt

½ cup capers, drained

1   Place all ingredients except capers into a large saucepan or preserving pan. Cook over a medium heat, stirring regularly until well reduced – this takes about 20-30 minutes.

2   Add capers and simmer for a further 5 minutes. Cool. This relish is best stored in the refrigerator – it cannot be bottled as it will ferment.

Makes about 2 cups

BEETROOT AND LEMON CHUTNEY

Vibrant in colour and with a stunning tangy flavour this chutney is truly delectable.

2 lemons

2 large raw beetroot, peeled and grated

1 large onion, peeled and diced

2 cups wine vinegar

2 cups raw sugar, firmly packed

3 cm piece fresh ginger, peeled and grated

2 tsp ground coriander

2 tsp ground cinnamon

1 tblsp salt

1 Cut lemons into quarters, slice thinly and discard seeds. Place into a saucepan, cover with water and simmer for about 15 minutes until tender.

2 Combine with remaining ingredients. Bring to the boil, stirring until sugar dissolves. Simmer uncovered, stirring occasionally for about 45 minutes until thick.

3 Pour hot chutney into sterilised jars and seal well.

Makes about 6 cups

LIME MARMALADE

Pale green and full of tang and zest!

1 kg limes

4 cups sugar

1 Cut limes into quarters, remove and reserve any seeds. Finely slice quarters. Place sliced limes and any juice into a bowl and cover with water. Place seeds into a piece of muslin, tie securely and add to limes. Allow to soak overnight.

2 Next day, pour lime mixture into a large saucepan or preserving pan. Boil gently until limes are softened and liquid reduced by about half – this will take about 30 minutes. Remove muslin bag.

3 Add sugar and stir until dissolved. Boil rapidly until setting point is reached (see raspberry jam, page 103). Skim any foam from surface. Allow to cool for 10 minutes then stir to evenly distribute fruit.

4 Ladle into sterilised jars and seal well.

Makes about 6 cups

GUAVA JELLY

An oldie but a goodie. Jellies are a bit of a palaver but they are well worth it.

1.5 kg guavas, roughly chopped
3-4 cups sugar
juice of 3 lemons

1   Place guavas into a preserving pan or large saucepan and cover with water. Bring to the boil then simmer for about 45 minutes until guavas are very soft. Remove from the heat, purée in a blender. Tip pulp into a scalded jelly bag or piece of muslin. Suspend over a non-metallic bowl and leave undisturbed overnight.

2   Next day measure the strained juice. Place guava and lemon juice into pan and add 1 cup sugar for every 1 cup of juice. Bring to the boil, stirring until sugar has dissolved. Boil hard until setting point is reached – this takes about 10-15 minutes (see raspberry jam, page 103).

3   Remove from the heat and skim any foam from surface. Ladle into hot sterilised jars and seal well.

Makes about 3 cups

APRICOT JAM

Exquisite piled onto a warmed croissant or toasted bagel in true café style.

1 kg ripe but firm apricots
zest and juice of one lemon
1 cup water
4 cups sugar

1   Halve the apricots, removing their stones. Place into a large saucepan or preserving pan with lemon zest, juice and water. Bring to the boil, then simmer until tender.

2   Add sugar and bring to the boil, stirring until sugar has dissolved. Boil hard until setting point is reached (see raspberry jam, page 103).

3   Remove from the heat and skim any foam from surface. Allow to cool for 10 minutes then stir to evenly distribute fruit. Ladle into hot sterilised jars and seal well.

Makes about 5 cups

TRY LUSCIOUS LEMON CURD WITH A BUTTERY
BRIOCHE, OR BY THE SPOONFUL IF YOU CAN'T RESIST

Lemon Curd

LEMON CURD

Try luscious lemon curd with a buttery brioche, or by the spoonful if you can't resist it.

125 g butter

1 cup sugar

finely grated rind and juice of 4
    lemons

3 large eggs, beaten

1. Place all ingredients except eggs into a double boiler. Stir over heat until sugar has dissolved and mixture is warm. Whisk warm mixture into beaten eggs. Strain through a non-metallic sieve and return to double boiler. Cook over a low heat until mixture thickens to coat the back of a spoon. Do not allow the mixture to boil or it will curdle. Pour into hot sterilised jars and seal well. Will keep for 3-4 weeks in a cool place.

Makes about 2 cups

RASPBERRY JAM

It may seem odd for people to go out to a café for breakfast and order toast but when the jam is this good, why not?

1 kg raspberries

3½ cups sugar

juice of one lemon

1. Layer berries and sugar in a non-metallic bowl, pour over juice and leave in a cool place overnight.

2. Next day, pour fruit mixture into a large saucepan or preserving pan. Heat gently until sugar dissolves. Bring quickly to the boil and boil rapidly for about 10-15 minutes or until setting point is reached. Test by placing a spoonful onto a chilled plate. If the sample wrinkles when pushed with a finger, the jam is ready to set.

3. Remove from the heat and skim any foam from the surface. Allow to cool for 10 minutes then stir to evenly distribute fruit.

4. Ladle into hot sterilised jars and seal well.

Makes about 4 cups

<u>11</u> SWEETS

Sweet food is there to amuse rather than appease the appetite but what delightful amusement it gives! Sweet treats are a big part of café fare. From small refreshments to enjoy with a morning cappuccino, to something more decadent later in the day, few can resist a sweet titbit. Making sweets can be a satisfying, almost therapeutic pastime. Think of them as something to cook for the sheer delight of cooking, rather than for culinary perfection.

LITTLE CHOCOLATE RAISIN CAKES

A big hit with chocolate raisin lovers. Believe it or not, these little cakes actually taste like a giant chocolate raisin!

125 g butter
200 g cooking chocolate
1 cup caster sugar
½ cup raisins, chopped
4 large eggs, beaten
1½ tblsp flour
½ cup chocolate-coated raisins

1. Preheat oven to 180°C. Line 6 extra-large muffin tins with circles of non-stick baking paper and grease well.
2. In a saucepan gently melt butter and chocolate, add sugar and stir to dissolve, add raisins. Carefully stir in beaten eggs and finally flour. Pour into prepared tins. Bake for 20 minutes. The cakes should still be a little soft in the centre. Cool slightly before carefully removing from tins. Serve topped with chocolate ganache (below) and chocolate-coated raisins.

Makes 6 little cakes

CHOCOLATE GANACHE

Ganache is a classic French preparation. Use hot as a smooth chocolate sauce or cold as icing.

½ cup dark chocolate melts
½ cup cream

1. Gently melt chocolate and cream in microwave or in a double boiler. Stir to form a smooth sauce. Allow to cool and thicken then spoon mounds onto each little cake.

Makes 1 cup

Little Chocolate Raisin Cakes

WILDLY POPULAR, THIS GOOEY LEMON SLICE
FORMS ITS OWN MERINGUE-LIKE CRUST

Lemon Slice

LEMON SLICE

Wildly popular, this gooey lemon slice forms its own meringue-like crust.

Crust:

1½ cups flour

¾ cup caster sugar

150 g butter, cubed

Filling:

4 large eggs

1¾ cups caster sugar

finely grated zest of 3 lemons

⅔ cup lemon juice (from about 4-5 lemons)

⅓ cup plain flour, sieved

icing sugar to dust

1 Preheat oven to 180°C. Line a 20 x 35 cm tin with non-stick baking paper.

2 Place flour and sugar into the bowl of a food processor, pulse to sift. Add butter and process to resemble fine breadcrumbs. Press crumbs evenly over base of prepared tin. Bake for 15 minutes until golden. Remove, reduce oven to 140°C.

Filling

1 Whisk eggs and sugar together until very thick and pale. Fold in lemon juice, zest then flour. Pour over crust and bake for 40 minutes or until set. Cool completely before cutting into squares. Serve dusted with icing sugar.

Makes 12 squares

CHOCOLATE BROWNIES

Try these for dessert – they're divine served hot with whipped cream.

250 g butter

250 g cooking chocolate

6 large eggs

2½ cups sugar

½ cup plain flour

½ cup cocoa powder

icing sugar to dust

Optional extras

½ cup toasted peanuts or hazelnuts

½ cup chocolate chips or bits, or white chocolate bits

½ cup raisins

1 Preheat oven to 160°C. Line a 20 x 35 cm tin with non-stick baking paper.

2 Melt butter and chocolate together in the microwave for 2-3 minutes, or in a double boiler. With an electric beater whisk whole eggs and sugar together until very thick and pale. Stir in melted butter and chocolate. Fold in sifted flour and cocoa. Pour into prepared tin. Bake for 1 hour or until a skewer inserted comes out clean. Cool, remove from tin and cut into slices. Serve sprinkled with icing sugar.

Makes 12 large pieces

MIXED BERRY COMPOTE

Frozen berries can easily be substituted for fresh in this colourful compote. Dollop it next to meringues, chocolate cake or whatever takes your fancy. In the café it is also very popular served with muesli in the morning.

2 tblsp cornflour

¾ cup water

juice of one lemon

¼ cup sugar

2 cups boysenberries

1 cup raspberries

1 cup strawberries

1   Blend cornflour with water, place into a saucepan with lemon juice and sugar. Bring to the boil whisking constantly until thickened and cornflour has cooked out. Add berries and cook gently until they just soften. Cool. Serve with meringues and cream.

Serves 4-6

MERINGUES

Meringues go well with cream, lemon curd, berry compote or just about anything!

3 egg whites

1 cup caster sugar

1   Preheat oven to 100°C. Whisk egg whites until stiff. Add 1 tablespoonful of the sugar and whisk until incorporated. Whisk in remaining sugar until mixture is glossy. Spoon or pipe small mounds onto an oven tray. Bake for 1½ hours.

Makes 20 small meringues

DOLLOP IT NEXT TO MERINGUES, CHOCOLATE
CAKE OR WHATEVER TAKES YOUR FANCY

Mixed Berry Compote and Meringues

TURKISH VELVET BISCUITS

Café-style biscuits – coffee, coffee and more coffee!

¼ cup finely ground coffee

1 cup caster sugar

150 g butter, softened

1 cup caster sugar

1 egg

1 tblsp strong espresso

¼ cup finely ground coffee

½ tsp baking soda

½ tsp ground allspice

1½ cups plain flour, sifted

chocolate-coated coffee beans
   (optional)

1 Mix first measure of ground coffee and sugar together and set to one side. Preheat oven to 175ºC. Lightly grease a baking tray.

2 Cream butter and sugar together until pale. Beat in egg, espresso, ground coffee, baking soda and allspice. Stir in flour to form a smooth dough. Form into walnut-sized balls, roll in coffee sugar (as above) to coat well. Place onto baking tray and flatten slightly. Bake 10 minutes until risen and firm.

3 Remove from tray to a cooling rack. Once cold top with a chocolate-coated coffee bean if desired – these can be stuck onto biscuits with a little melted chocolate.

Makes 3-4 dozen, depending on size

BLACKBERRY FRANGIPANE TART

Any berries enhance this tart and frozen berries are fine if fresh are unavailable.

300 g sweet shortcrust
   pastry (see page 112)

125 g butter, softened

½ cup caster sugar

2 eggs

2 drops almond essence
   (optional)

1½ cups ground almonds

1 tblsp flour

3 tblsp blackberry jam

2 punnets fresh blackberries
   (or 1½ cup frozen berries)

icing sugar to dust

1 Roll pastry on a lightly floured board to 3 mm thick, line a 24 cm tart tin. Chill well.

2 Preheat oven to 175ºC. Cream butter and sugar, add egg and beat well. Stir in essence, ground almonds and flour to form a paste.

3 Spread jam in base of tart shell, cover with almond paste, sprinkle evenly with blackberries. Bake for 45 minutes or until golden and well set in the middle. Serve hot or cold, dusted with icing sugar.

Serves 6-8

CAFÉ-STYLE BISCUITS – COFFEE,
COFFEE AND MORE COFFEE!

Turkish Velvet Biscuits

ORANGE POPPY SEED CAKE

A very 'cakey' cake. Luscious soaking in a wet, tart orange syrup that complements the sandy texture and aromatic flavour of the poppy seeds.

175 g butter, softened

1½ cups caster sugar

2 tblsp finely grated orange zest

4 large eggs

½ cup low-fat yoghurt

½ cup orange juice

1½ cups plain flour

½ cup poppy seeds

½ tsp baking soda

Orange syrup:

1 cup orange juice

½ cup lemon juice

2 tblsp julienne orange zest

½ cup sugar

1   Preheat oven to 160°C. Grease and flour a 20 cm kugelhopf tin.

2   Cream butter and sugar until pale. Add zest and eggs one by one, beating well. Fold in yoghurt and orange juice. Sift in flour, baking soda and poppy seeds, fold to combine. Pour into prepared cake tin. Bake for 50 minutes or until a skewer inserted comes out clean. Allow to stand for 10 minutes before turning out.

Serves 8-10

Orange Syrup

1   Place all ingredients into a saucepan. Bring to the boil then simmer until thick and syrupy. Pour hot syrup over poppy seed cake to serve.

SWEET SHORTCRUST PASTRY

This pastry is very forgiving, patches well if necessary and cooks to a lovely crisp, golden crust. Wrap pastry in plastic wrap, store in refrigerator for up to 1 week or in freezer for up to 3 months.

250 g butter, softened

¾ cup caster sugar

1 egg

3 cups plain flour

1   Beat butter, sugar and egg together to just combine but do not cream mixture. Gently mix in flour to form a dough. Wrap in plastic wrap, refrigerate ½ hour or until firm enough to roll out.

2   Use as recipe directs.

Makes 850 g, enough to produce 2-3 sweet tart recipes

LUSCIOUS SOAKING IN A WET, TART ORANGE SYRUP
THAT COMPLEMENTS THE SANDY TEXTURE AND
AROMATIC FLAVOUR OF THE POPPY SEEDS

Orange Poppy Seed Cake

THE PRETTIEST THING YOU EVER DID SEE
AND A LIGHT PUFF OF AIR TO EAT!

Lemon Berry Pavlova Roulade

LEMON BERRY PAVLOVA ROULADE

The prettiest thing you ever did see and a light puff of air to eat!

6 egg whites

1½ cups caster sugar

1 tblsp lemon juice

finely grated zest of one lemon

Filling:

1 punnet raspberries

1 cup cream, whipped

¼ cup caster sugar

2 tblsp limoncello liqueur or any other preferred liqueur (optional)

icing sugar to dust

fresh raspberries to serve

1 Preheat oven to 160°C. Line a sponge roll tin with non-stick baking paper.

2 Whisk egg whites until firm peaks hold. Add sugar a little at a time, continue beating until glossy and sugar has dissolved. Fold in juice and zest. Spread into prepared tin and bake for 20 minutes.

3 Remove from oven, allow to cool for 10 minutes before turning out onto a clean tea towel sprinkled with caster sugar.

4 When cold, spread with filling and roll up. Refrigerate to set for a couple of hours. Dust with icing sugar if desired and serve with fresh raspberries.

Filling

1 Crush raspberries and gently fold all ingredients together.

Serves 10

GOOSEBERRY TARTLETS

Green gooseberries turn a pretty pink when cooked with sugar.

Pastry:

350 g sweet shortcrust pastry (see recipe page 112)

Filling:

3 cups green gooseberries

1½ cups sugar

juice of one lemon

¼ cup water

1 Roll out pastry to 3 mm thick and line six 10 cm tartlet tins, chill well.

2 Place filling ingredients into a saucepan. Bring to the boil, stirring until sugar dissolves. Boil gently until berries burst and mixture becomes syrupy. Cool.

3 Preheat oven to 200°C. Spoon filling into prepared pastry cases. Bake for 15 minutes until pastry is golden.

Makes 6

PLUM FRIANDS

The plums can be replaced with any other seasonal fruit. Even plain, these little almond cakes are very French – moist, sweet pieces of heaven.

175 g butter, melted

1 cup ground almonds

6 egg whites, lightly beaten

1½ cups icing sugar

½ cup plain flour

6 plums, halved, stones removed

1   Preheat oven to 180ºC. Grease a 12-hole muffin pan.

2   Place all ingredients except plums into a mixing bowl. Stir until just combined. Pour mixture into muffin pans – they should be about ½ full. Top each friand with half a plum. Bake for 25 minutes.

3   Allow to stand in pans for 5 minutes before turning out onto a cooling rack.

Makes 12

COCONUT MACAROON CAKE

A crisp crust encircles this gooey coconut cake. Do not overcook or it will loose its unique and deliciously sticky consistency.

Crust:

2½ cups ground almonds

½ cup caster sugar

½ cup flour

150g butter, cubed

Filling:

6 eggs

2 cups caster sugar

4 cups desiccated coconut

1 tblsp butter, melted

2 tsp vanilla essence

1   Preheat oven to 160ºC. Grease a 26 cm springform cake tin.

2   Place ground almonds, sugar and flour into the bowl of a food processor. Pulse to sift. Add butter and process until crumbly. Press into base and sides of cake tin. Chill well.

3   To make filling, whisk eggs and sugar together until very thick and pale. Gently fold in remaining ingredients. Pour into chilled base. Bake for 1½ hours until set. Cool well before removing from cake tin.

Serves 12

117

EVEN PLAIN, THESE LITTLE ALMOND CAKES ARE
VERY FRENCH – MOIST, SWEET PIECES OF HEAVEN

Plum Friands

SWEET MOIST PEARS AND SPICY GINGERBREAD ARE A SUBLIME COMBINATION

Pear and Gingerbread Upside-down Cake with
Maple Biscuit Semifreddo

PEAR AND GINGERBREAD UPSIDE-DOWN CAKE

Sweet moist pears and spicy gingerbread are a sublime combination. Serve with a half-and-half blend of yoghurt and whipped cream for a combined taste sensation.

Topping:

120 g butter, softened

1 cup soft brown sugar

4-5 pears, cored and sliced

Cake batter:

2 cups plain flour

1 tsp baking soda

½ tsp salt

2 tblsp ground cinnamon

1 tblsp ground ginger

1 tsp ground nutmeg

1 tsp ground cloves

2 cups brown sugar

3 large eggs, beaten

1 cup buttermilk

125 g butter, melted

1 Preheat oven to 160°C. Grease a 26 cm springform cake tin.

2 Cream topping butter and sugar together and smooth into base of prepared cake tin. Arrange pear slices attractively over creamed base.

3 Place dry ingredients into a large bowl. Make a well in the centre and pour in eggs, buttermilk and melted butter. Gently mix to form a smooth batter. Pour cake batter over base. Bake for 1½ hours or until cake is firm and a skewer inserted comes out clean.

Serves 12

MAPLE BISCUIT SEMIFREDDO

Semifreddo will never freeze completely solid – its name means 'half cold' and it is meant to be soft and creamy. Try using crushed gingernuts, amaretti or even malt biscuits for a change in flavour.

125 g crushed wine biscuits

1 cup cream

½ cup maple syrup

2 egg whites

2 tblsp brandy

1 Crush biscuits. Whip cream and maple syrup together until just holding shape. In a clean bowl whisk egg whites to soft peaks.

2 Gently fold crushed biscuits, cream, egg whites and brandy together. Pour mixture into a freezer-proof container. Freeze for 24 hours.

Serves 4-6

VANILLA and APRICOT BREAD and BUTTER PUDDING CAKE

A pudding set into cake form! For a subtle change in texture, try using stale brioches or croissants instead of bread. Let your imagination go wild and vary the flavours – substitute chocolate and espresso or maybe rum and raisin for the vanilla and apricots.

100 g butter, softened

10 slices white sandwich bread, halved

1 cup chopped dried apricots

½ cup brown sugar, tightly packed

5 large eggs

pinch salt

2 cups milk

½ cup cream

1 tblsp vanilla essence

½ cup dry sherry

1 tblsp caster sugar

1 Grease a 20 cm springform cake tin. Butter bread and layer in prepared tin alternating with apricots and brown sugar. Press down well. Make sure top layer of bread is attractively arranged.

2 Beat eggs, salt, milk, cream, vanilla, sherry and sugar together. Pour evenly over cake and leave to rest for ½ hour for bread to completely absorb liquid. Preheat oven to 150ºC.

3 Cover with cooking foil and bake for 30 minutes. Remove foil and bake for a further 30 minutes. Cake will inflate slightly when cooked, deflating again once it is cold. Allow to cool a little before removing from tin. Serve warm or cold.

Serves 12

A PUDDING SET INTO CAKE FORM!

Vanilla and Apricot Bread
and Butter Pudding Cake

CHOCOLATE PRUNE TRUFFLES

Wickedly rich and seductive, these are the perfect little luxury to accompany a good coffee.

½ cup pitted prunes, chopped

2 tblsp brandy

50 g butter

¼ cup cream

250 g dark chocolate

1 egg yolk

sifted cocoa to roll

1 Put prunes and brandy in a bowl to macerate for 1 hour.

2 Melt butter, cream and chocolate together, whisking until smooth. Add yolk, prunes and brandy, stir to combine. Chill until set. Form into small balls, roll in cocoa. Keep in the refrigerator until ready to serve.

Makes about 40

PASSIONFRUIT and WHITE CHOCOLATE CHEESECAKE

A smooth intense cheesecake full of passion and fruit and flavour.

Base:

250 g packet wine biscuits

¼ cup caster sugar

125 g butter, melted

Cheesecake filling:

300 g cream cheese

3 tblsp caster sugar

3 large eggs

300 g white chocolate melts

300 ml cream

½ cup passionfruit pulp

fresh passionfruit to serve

1 Preheat oven to 150°C. Grease a 26 cm springform cake tin.

2 Place wine biscuits and sugar in the bowl of a food processor. Process to crush biscuits. Pour in melted butter, pulse to combine. Press mixture into the base of prepared tin. Chill.

3 Beat cream cheese and sugar together until smooth. Add eggs one at a time.

4 Gently melt white chocolate and cream together in the microwave or over a double boiler, stir until smooth then beat into cream cheese mixture. Stir in passionfruit. Pour over prepared base.

5 Bake for 1 hour until set. Cool. Slice with a wet knife. Serve with fresh passionfruit.

Serves 12

WICKEDLY RICH AND SEDUCTIVE, THESE ARE THE PERFECT
LITTLE LUXURY TO ACCOMPANY A GOOD COFFEE

Chocolate Prune Truffles

PARSNIP CAKE IS POSSIBLY EVEN NICER THAN THE
CLASSIC CARROT CAKE ON WHICH IT IS BASED

Parsnip Cake

PARSNIP CAKE

Parsnip cake is possibly even nicer than the classic carrot cake on which it is based. Parsnips are very high in natural sugars and these caramelise to give this cake an amazing flavour.

1 cup caster sugar

1¼ cups vegetable oil

1 tsp vanilla essence

3 large eggs

½ cup crushed pineapple

4 cups grated parsnip

1⅓ cups plain flour

½ tsp salt

1 tsp baking soda

½ cup currants

2 tblsp ground cinnamon

1   Preheat oven to 160°C. Grease a 20 cm springform cake tin.

2   Whisk sugar, oil and vanilla together to combine. Add eggs one at a time, beating until mixture is creamy. Stir in pineapple.

3   Place grated parsnip, flour, salt, baking soda, currants and cinnamon in a large bowl. Pour in the wet mixture, stir to combine. Spoon cake mixture into prepared tin. Bake for 1½ hours or until a skewer inserted comes out clean. Once cold, ice with lemon cream cheese icing.

Serves 12

Lemon cream cheese icing:

1 cup cream cheese, softened

50 g butter, melted

½ cup caster sugar

grated rind and juice of one lemon

Lemon cream cheese icing

1   Beat all ingredients together until creamy. Spread over cake.

PISTACHIO BISCOTTI

Double-baked biscuits can be seen being dunked into strong espresso in respectable cafés at any time of the day.

2 eggs

⅔ cup caster sugar

finely grated zest of one lemon

½ cup pistachio nuts, toasted

½ cup ground almonds

1 tsp baking powder

plain flour

extra caster sugar

1   Preheat oven to 170°C. Whisk eggs and sugar until very thick and pale. Stir in lemon zest, pistachios, ground almonds and baking powder. Add enough flour to form a firm paste.

2   Shape paste into 2 logs and place onto a lightly greased oven tray. Sprinkle with caster sugar. Bake for 20 minutes or until golden and firm. Remove and cool a little then cut into 1 cm slices. Spread slices onto baking tray; reduce oven temperature to 140°C and bake for 30 minutes until dry. Store in an airtight container.

Makes about 40

INDEX